Unapologetic Self-Love

Self-Worth and Empowerment Workbook To Build
Self-Esteem, Inner Strength, and Personal Growth
Through Self-Compassion

Rebecca Brady

Pages By The Lake, LLC

Contents

Introduction

Every one of us has the hope of becoming the best version of ourselves. Yet, somewhere along the way, many of us lose sight of who we truly are. We are confronted with doubts and insecurities, and often subconsciously carry forward wounds from our past that compromise our self-perception. But with that comes the desire to heal, thrive, and reclaim our joy. To do that, we have to embrace a key concept: self-love.

Self-love may seem like an indulgence, but it isn't; it's a necessity for a fulfilling life. Self-love is the bedrock for emotional well-being, happiness, and personal growth. When you nurture yourself—mind, body, and soul—you open the door to incredible possibilities like growth, healing, and real connections with others. But in a world rife with misconceptions, self-love is frequently misunderstood.

Often labeled as selfishness or mistaken for narcissism, self-love is burdened by societal myths that undermine its true essence. It's typical to worry that embracing self-love might lead to becoming self-centered and abandoning relationships or responsibilities. However, the reality is quite the opposite. Genuine self-love develops compassion, empathy, and an understanding of how we connect to each other. As we heal and become whole within ourselves, we can better support those around us, forming stronger, more meaningful connections.

This book is born from a desire to redefine how we perceive caring for ourselves. In my previous work, *Breaking Free From the Grip of Toxic Parenting*, I focused on the "why" behind our emotional responses and how to stop them. Now, it's time to explore the "how" of thriving after surviving. How do we build ourselves up once we've stepped away from toxic influences? How do we turn survival into a full life?

In the pages ahead, prepare to get to know yourself like never before! It will be a voyage filled with ups and downs, challenges and triumphs. Self-love is dynamic and requires patience, courage, and continual effort. But with strategies to transform self-doubt into confidence, you will recognize that each step—even the tiny ones—contributes to your personal growth.

This book is an invitation to reconnect with your real self, the one that might have gotten lost somewhere inside you as you overcame previous experiences. Together, we will explore practical tools and actionable strategies designed to support your path towards self-acceptance and love. You'll learn how to see beauty in imperfection, to celebrate your strengths, and to face your fears with resilience.

But you aren't alone; we will also **take a look at stories from those who once grappled with feeling unworthy or overwhelmed by doubt.** These shared experiences illustrate that you can rely on the strength of others. As someone who has walked this road, I can attest to the fact that self-love is a lifelong endeavor. It is my hope that you will have reclaimed elements of your identity that were once lost by the time you reach the end of this book. That you will recognize the immense value that lies within you, deserving of joy, fulfillment, and peace. Self-love is not about perfecting yourself, but rather about embracing every part of who you are, unapologetically.

It's time to unravel the constraints that hold you back and move boldly toward a future that celebrates who you are, in all your flawed and glorious humanity. Open your heart to this process of self-discovery, and take confident steps toward reclaiming your joy, defining your growth, and ultimately, loving yourself fully and fiercely.

Chapter One

The Root of Self-Doubt

Self-doubt can feel like an uninvited guest. It lurks in your mind and clouds your self-perception. In this chapter, we consider the roots of self-doubt and explore how it often stems from past experiences, societal expectations, and critical inner voices. While you may have already identified the origins of your self-doubt, our focus here is on living your best life beyond that awareness. True transformation occurs when you shift your mindset from limitation to empowerment. Through introspection and practical strategies, you will learn how to break down the walls that self-doubt builds and empower yourself with a sense of resilience.

Identifying Negative Thought Patterns

Negative thought patterns are recurring, irrational beliefs that distort your perception of reality. They tend to appear as automatic thoughts, such as "I'm not good enough" or "My past defines me." These thoughts can create a cycle of self-doubt that undermines your confidence and well-being. Focusing on these negative beliefs can ingrain them in your mind and influence how you view yourself and your abilities. This constant barrage of negativity can lead to a sense of helplessness and anxiety that makes it challenging to love your true self. Recognizing and challenging these patterns allows you to break free from their hold and adopt a healthier mindset.

Common Negative Thoughts

Negative thoughts might pop up more than we like to admit; they often sneak into our minds when we least expect them. These thoughts can be harsh and unforgiving, manifesting as beliefs like "I'm not worthy," "I'll never succeed," or "I don't belong." Knowing that these thoughts are prevalent can reduce their power over you. They happen automatically and unconsciously, but realizing this can help you break free from them. Many times, you might not even realize when you're engaging in negative self-talk. It shows up as negativity, self-criticism, and doubting yourself. Identifying these thoughts is the first step toward challenging their validity. Become more aware of your thought patterns to take control of your inner dialogue and create space for positive affirmations and self-acceptance.

Acknowledging your negative thought patterns enables personal growth. It takes courage to confront the beliefs that hold you back, but doing so empowers you to change. When you notice negative thoughts, pause and validate your feelings. It's okay to experience self-doubt; what matters is how you respond. A thought diary is a great place to capture negative thoughts as they arise. This practice helps you recognize them without judgment and reflects your commitment to self-improvement. We will discuss strategies to overcome negative self-talk in Chapter 3.

Patterns of Self-Criticism

Self-criticism—which is part of negative thinking—creates a cycle that feeds on itself, resulting in a detrimental impact on your self-esteem. You might start with a small mistake or a perceived flaw, and before you know it, this tiny crack turns into a chasm of self-doubt. You might think, "I should have done better," which leads to feelings of inadequacy and shame. This snowballs until you are beating yourself up about nothing, and all that does is ruin your self-perception.

The cycle of self-criticism can affect your daily life and decision-making. Self-criticism can hinder your ability to make choices aligned with your values and desires. As you criticize yourself, you begin to make decisions out of fear rather than empowerment. Self-criticism often stems from unmet expectations. The best thing you can do is self-reflection.

Ask yourself:

- Are these expectations realistic? Where do they come from?

- What beliefs or experiences have shaped these expectations?

- How would I feel if I let go of these expectations entirely?

- What alternative outcomes or paths could lead to fulfillment beyond my current expectations?

The answers to these questions allow you to unpack your personal narratives, which opens doors to new perspectives. Challenge yourself to shift from self-criticism to self-kindness. Instead of saying, "I always mess up," try saying, "I made a mistake, but I can learn from it." This small change can lead to changes in how you view yourself.

Mindset Traps

Mindset traps are mental patterns that create barriers to growth, which may cause self-doubt. Common mindset traps include:

- All-or-nothing thinking: Seeing situations in black-and-white terms.,

- Discounting the positive: Only focusing on what went wrong.

- Overgeneralization: Drawing broad conclusions based on a single negative experience.

- Catastrophizing: Assuming the worst possible outcome in any given situation.

- Mind Reading: Assuming you know what others are thinking and believing that they view you negatively.

- Emotional Reasoning: Believing that negative emotions reflect your reality.

Overcome these traps by adopting a growth mindset. With a growth mindset, you embrace challenges and see failures as opportunities for learning. This contrasts with a fixed mindset, which clings to the belief that abilities and intelligence cannot change.

As you work through self-doubt using a growth mindset, think about the concept of liberation. What would it feel like to let go of limiting beliefs? Small mindset shifts—such as reminding yourself of past successes or re-framing setbacks as learning opportunities—can have a massive impact on your outlook. Liberation opens pathways to self-compassion and lets you treat yourself with kindness and understanding.

The Impact of Labels

Self-imposed labels can limit your individuality and perpetuate doubt. Whether it's "I am a failure," "I am not creative," or any label that defines you narrowly, these narratives often overshadow your true potential. These labels are not fixed truths about your identity, and when you realize that, you begin to see the possibility of change.

Reflect on the labels you've given yourself: Are they serving you well? What would you rather be known for? Challenge any labels that feel restrictive, and consider alternatives that celebrate your growth and uniqueness. Unlabeling yourself helps you experience personal growth, which offers hope.

The Impact of Overthinking and Comparison

Overthinking is the process of excessively analyzing situations, decisions, or feelings. When you overthink, your mind races with "what if" scenarios, making it difficult to take action or find peace. It's like you are stuck in a constant cycle of going through different scenarios but never making a decision. Comparison, on the other hand, occurs when you measure your worth against others, which leads to feelings of inadequacy or self-doubt. Both overthinking and comparison feed self-doubt.

Overthinking

Overthinking is a mental process where you continuously analyze things, often resulting in excessive worry and indecision. It can create a swirling storm of thoughts in your mind and make it challenging to find clarity. Overthinking is not the same as reflecting; You're ruminating, stuck in a cycle of "what if" scenarios that can amplify your self-doubt. It's like a car stuck in neutral—although the engine is running, you're not moving forward.

Overthinking can affect you in several ways:

- In relationships, the fear of making mistakes or looking foolish can lead to second-guessing yourself and your decisions.

- It can result in analysis paralysis, where the fear of making the wrong choice prevents you from making any choice at all.

- You may find yourself caught in a loop of self-doubt, replaying conversations or actions, which makes you exhausted and overwhelmed.

Chronic overthinking creates a relentless cycle that reinforces your self-doubt and anxiety. As you analyze a situation from multiple angles, you may focus on perceived flaws or shortcomings, which magnifies your feelings of inadequacy. This cycle can make challenges seem insurmountable and leave you paralyzed by fear and uncertainty. Before you know it, you're spiraling deeper into a pit of doubt, questioning your decisions and worth.

Break free from this detrimental cycle by taking action, even if it seems small. For example, physical activity, mindfulness, or setting a timer for short decision-making periods can disrupt the cycle of overthinking. You could commit to making one small decision each day without going back and analyzing it endlessly. These small actions let you regain a sense of control and move toward empowerment.

Comparison Traps

Social media perpetuates harmful comparisons. Curated posts showcase the highlights of others' lives, making it easy to feel inadequate in comparison. You might scroll through perfectly staged images and thoughts, and you end up measuring your worth against others. This often results in a distorted self-image, as social media reality can be far removed from actual experiences.

Societal expectations further fuel these comparisons. You may feel pressured to achieve milestones like career success, relationships, or even physical appearance based on what you see around you. This constant barrage of information can make you feel inferior and prompt you to question your journey. Accept, right now, that each person's journey is unique. What you see online is often an edited version of reality and doesn't encompass the struggles and challenges others face, so it doesn't help to compare yourself with them. Embracing your unique path allows you to appreciate your accomplishments without the shadow of comparison looming over you.

It may be helpful to practice gratitude for your journey. Start a gratitude journal where you write down aspects of your life you appreciate, including your growth and resilience. Reflecting on your experiences helps to move your focus away from what others are doing and toward acknowledging your successes.

Consequences of Comparing

The emotional toll of constant comparisons on your self-esteem and self-worth can be severe. When you compare yourself to others, you diminish your accomplishments, leading to feelings of loneliness and dissatisfaction. You might feel as though your efforts go unnoticed or that you don't measure up, which can cause a sense of disconnection from both yourself and others. These comparisons add to the cycle of negative self-talk. Constantly feeling like you're falling short can affect your motivation and outlook on life. You may become increasingly self-critical or believe that your worth is tied to how you measure up against others, which is fundamentally untrue.

Each person's path is valuable and worthy of recognition. Honor your personal achievements to help build your confidence. Reflect on your successes, even the tiny ones, and celebrate them. Sett aside time to acknowledge what you've accomplished in a week, month, or year. Create a habit of recognizing your efforts without immediately downplaying them.

By focusing on honoring your story, you learn to appreciate your unique contributions to the world. Start by creating a list of your accomplishments—areas where you've grown or overcome obstacles—and revisit it whenever you find yourself slipping into comparison. This practice of self-recognition reinforces the idea that your journey is valuable and independent of others' paths.

Strategies for Overcoming Comparison

It takes conscious effort to stop comparisons. The following practical strategies can help you reclaim your focus.

Limited Exposure

Limit your exposure to anything that causes you to compare yourself to others. This could mean consciously reducing your time on social media, taking breaks, or unfollowing accounts that trigger feelings of inadequacy. Curate your feed to include positive influences and surround yourself with accounts that encourage and uplift rather than those that make you feel less than.

Self-Reflection

Self-reflection helps you recognize your individual growth points. Journal about your thoughts, values, and experiences. Reflect on questions like, "What are my goals?" and "What does success look like for me?" Implement a daily or weekly reflection practice where you document your achievements and feelings. It will help you build self-awareness and reinforce the importance of acknowledging your unique journey.

Positive Affirmations

Positive affirmations can be added to your day to reinforce your self-worth. Here is how you can develop a list of affirmations that resonate with you

1. Reflect on aspects of your life where you feel self-doubt or negativity. Determine the specific areas you want to address, such as self-worth, confidence, or resilience.

2. Turn your areas of improvement into positive affirmations. Use empowering language that asserts your abilities and values. For example, if you struggle with self-worth, you might say, "I am

worthy of love and respect."

3. Phrase your affirmations as if they are already true by using the present tense to reinforce the belief in your affirmations. For instance, instead of saying, "I will be confident," say, "I am confident."

4. Make your affirmations clear and specific to enhance their effectiveness. Instead of a vague statement, specify what confidence means to you, like, "I speak up for myself in conversations."

5. Repeat your affirmations aloud, write them down, or display them where you can see them often. Consistency will help reinforce these positive beliefs over time.

Applying these strategies allows you to create a more supportive environment for your personal growth. Overcoming the traps of overthinking and comparison is a process, and it's okay to take small steps; just keep going. The focus should be on nurturing your unique journey and celebrating your progress. Along the way, you'll find more peace and self-acceptance.

How Self-Judgment Develops

Self-judgment is the process of evaluating your thoughts, feelings, and actions with harsh criticism and negative scrutiny. It emerges from internalized beliefs, societal expectations, or past experiences, which lead you to question your worth and capabilities. You may find yourself focusing on perceived flaws and shortcomings rather than recognizing your strengths and achievements. This critical inner voice can create feelings of inadequacy and shame, resulting in a cycle of self-doubt and anxiety.

Sources of Self-Judgment

Self-judgment develops from various factors, including:

Upbringing

Your early experiences may affect your critical inner narrative. For instance, if you were raised in an environment that emphasized perfection or comparison, you might carry forward those expectations into adulthood. The messages you absorbed from family, friends, and educators can create a baseline of self-assessment that may be harsher than warranted.

Cultural and Social Factors

Cultural and social conditioning further affect unrealistic standards and encourage you to evaluate yourself against often unattainable benchmarks. These societal expectations can cause a sense of inadequacy and lead you to judge yourself harshly for not measuring up. Awareness of how these external factors shape your self-view helps to understand the context of your current feelings.

Fear of Judgment

Self-judgment might be rooted in a fear of judgment from others. You may worry about how your choices or failures are perceived, and that can lead to an internal dialogue filled with self-criticism. This fear is a common experience for many who have had a traumatic past, and recognizing that this is the case may nurture self-compassion; you are not alone in grappling with these feelings.

Consequences of Harsh Judgment

The impacts of self-judgment on emotional health and self-worth can be immense and far-reaching. Self-criticism often leads to heightened anxiety and depression. The constant feeling of unworthiness can create a heavy emotional burden that hampers your ability to enjoy life fully. This state of mind makes it crucial to address self-judgment, as it stunts personal growth and healing.

Harsh self-assessment can rob you of motivation and joy, which decreases your capacity to pursue opportunities and relationships. When you see yourself through a lens of judgment, it can limit your willingness to take risks or try new things, reinforcing negative patterns (Pearson and Wilson, 2024). In contrast, practicing compassionate self-reflection can change your emotional state. You become kind to yourself, which strengthens your self-worth and enriches your relationships, leading to improved emotional resilience.

It helps to understand the consequences of self-judgment, as it encourages you to welcome self-kindness. The idea is to treat yourself with the same compassion you extend to others, thereby developing a healthier and more supportive mindset.

Shifting Perspectives

Changing how you perceive yourself is a gradual process that requires intention and practice. You can re-evaluate self-judgment by replacing it with curiosity. Instead of criticizing yourself for making a mistake, ask questions like, "What can I learn from this experience?" or "Why do I feel this way?" This shift helps create a more supportive internal dialogue and welcomes growth.

Exploring the origin of your self-judgment can also give you valuable insights into personal patterns. You can journal about instances when you've judged yourself harshly. Reflect on the thought processes behind these judgments and their origins. Think back to how these judgments and emotions may relate to what happened in the past. Understanding why you think this way can help you unravel deep-seated beliefs and feelings of inadequacy.

As you reflect, keep in mind that everyone makes mistakes; this is part of being human. Whenever you catch yourself in a cycle of self-judgment, remind yourself that each misstep is an opportunity for learning and development. Think about what you can learn from the situation rather than dwelling on negative thoughts and self-judgment.

Moving Toward Self-Acceptance

Reducing the habit of self-judgment opens you up to greater self-acceptance. The road to self-compassion is filled with ups and downs, but with patience and practice, you can develop a more loving relationship with yourself.

Here are some self-acceptance techniques:

- Self-Affirmations: Create a list of affirmations that resonate with your true self, such as "I am enough," "I deserve love and kindness," and "I celebrate who I am." Repeat these affirmations to reinforce self-appreciation and gradually shift your internal dialogue away from criticism.

- Journaling or Introspective Writing: Set aside time each day to articulate your thoughts and feelings without judgment. Allow your emotions to flow freely onto the pages, which helps you process experiences and understand your emotions better.

- Celebrate Successes: It's easy to overlook minor victories, but recognizing them can be a powerful boost to your self-worth. Reflect on your achievements regularly and celebrate even the small steps in your journey. This consistent reinforcement of positive experiences nurtures a mindset of growth and confidence.

Implement these steps gradually, and you will find yourself experiencing greater self-acceptance and less self-judgment. The road to self-compassion is filled with ups and downs, but with patience and practice, you can develop a more loving relationship with yourself. Every step taken toward understanding and acceptance is a victory worth celebrating.

Key Takeaways

Overcoming self-doubt doesn't happen overnight. It takes time and an exploration of self. Understanding the roots of your self-doubt is the first step toward reclaiming your identity and emotional well-being. The insights you gain are your tools, empowering you to challenge negative beliefs and create a more positive narrative about yourself. Thriving after self-discovery requires ongoing practice, patience, and self-compassion. Celebrate your progress and embrace the future with an open heart. Trust in your resilience and the power of your choices. You are capable of nurturing your self-worth, so that you can flourish unapologetically as the unique and beautiful individual you are.

Chapter Two

Embracing Your True Self

Loving yourself—the good and bad—starts with acknowledging who you are, beyond the layers of expectations and fears. It's normal to feel the pressure to conform, especially from society, but in this chapter, we forget about what others think and focus on the essence of your identity: your values, passions, and quirks that make you uniquely you. It's time to shed the masks you wear and the narratives that no longer serve you. You empower yourself to live with intention and confidence when you embrace your authentic self. True fulfillment arises from breaking away from the mold and celebrating your individuality. In the following sections, you'll learn how to move away from self-doubt and step into a more joyful existence.

Self-Discovery Exercises to Find Your Identity

Self-discovery is the process of uncovering and understanding who you are at your core. It requires examining your beliefs, values, interests, and experiences to discover the qualities that shape your identity. Self-discovery empowers you to make choices that align with your authentic self, leading to a more fulfilling life. It helps you learn to recognize your strengths and passions, which helps you overcome challenges with resilience.

Journal About Your Life

Journaling is a structured approach to reflect on your experiences and uncover your core values. Writing about your day-to-day life, thoughts, and feelings creates a safe space for deeper self-understanding.

Use the following steps to journal for self-discovery:

1. Dedicate a specific time each day or week to journal.

2. Write freely and without judgment. Don't worry about grammar or coherence; simply let your thoughts flow.

3. Reflect on experiences by choosing specific events that impacted you. How did they make you feel? What lessons did you learn?

4. After journaling, read through your entries. Look for recurring themes or values that resonate with you, such as honesty, creativity, or compassion. Write these down.

5. Summarize your core values in a short statement. It will guide your decisions and actions moving forward, aligning your life with what matters to you.

Reflective writing gives you clarity and allows you to recognize aspects of yourself that may have been hidden beneath the surface, giving you a sense of purpose and fulfillment.

Personality Assessments

Personality assessments are tools that provide insights into your personality traits, revealing hidden strengths and preferences. These insights inform your decisions, relationships, and overall direction in life.

Follow this method to use personality assessments effectively:

1. Research and select reputable personality assessments, such as the Myers-Briggs Type Indicator (MBTI), the Enneagram, or the Big Five personality traits.

2. Complete the assessments honestly. Be open and honest in your responses for more accurate results.

3. Once you receive your results, reflect on what they mean. What traits stand out? How do they align with how you see yourself?

4. Use your assessment results to pinpoint your strengths, weaknesses, and preferences. How can these insights help you make informed life choices?

5. Think about how you can use these insights to explore new opportunities for personal growth.

Personality assessments can open doors to understanding who you are at a deeper level and enable you to build a life that reflects your identity and aspirations.

Creative Expression

Being creative is a beautiful way to discover more about yourself. You could use art, music, or dance to communicate your innermost feelings beyond words.

Here's how to do it:

1. Experiment with various forms of creative expression, such as painting, writing music, dancing, or crafting. Find what resonates with you.

2. Choose a space where you feel comfortable expressing yourself freely, like a quiet corner at home, a local park, or anywhere that inspires you.

3. Create without an end goal in mind. Focus on the process, rather than the final product. This can liberate you from personal and societal expectations.

4. After creating, reflect on how you felt during the process. What emotions emerged? Did any new passions or interests come to light?

5. If you feel comfortable, share your creative work with others. Their feedback may reveal insights about yourself that you hadn't considered before.

Artistic activities can ignite a sense of joy and provide relief from the pressure to conform, which unlocks layers of your identity that have been waiting to be discovered.

Mindful Reflection

Mindfulness can help you become attuned to your real feelings and desires. Becoming aware of your thoughts and emotions—without judging them at all—can teach you to accept yourself fully.

Spend some time in mindful reflection:

1. Begin with a few minutes of focused breathing. Inhale deeply, hold your breath for a moment, then exhale slowly. Deep breathing grounds you in the present moment.

2. Observe your thoughts as they arise, but do not judge them. Ask yourself where they come from. Are they rooted in fear or self-doubt? Acknowledge them, then let them pass, almost like releasing a balloon from your grip and watching it float away.

3. Check in with how you're feeling physically and emotionally. What sensations are present in your body? What emotions are you experiencing? Validate these feelings.

4. After your mindfulness session, reflect on your experience. What did you notice about yourself? Were there any surprising insights?

5. Implement mindfulness into your daily routine to increase your acceptance of yourself. You can do it through meditation, yoga, or taking a walk in nature; do what works for you.

Mindful reflection can help you dissolve layers of self-doubt and fear, allowing your true self to emerge more vividly.

Celebrate Your Individuality and Unique Strengths

Nurture self-love and boost your confidence by embracing your individuality and tapping into your strengths. What makes you different validates your worth and infuses your life with authenticity. Celebrating your unique qualities frees you from the fear of judgment and empowers you to chase your passions and dreams. These strengths increase your resilience and self-assurance, equipping you to deal with challenges confidently. This creates a positive cycle, which increases your sense of belonging and purpose.

Identify Your Strengths

A structured approach can be used to recognize your talents and qualities. Take the time to reflect on what you excel at, and you lay a solid foundation for empowerment and self-worth.

Here's how to identify your strengths:

1. Think about past experiences and moments when you felt proud or accomplished. What skills did you use? What qualities helped you succeed?

2. Ask friends, family, or colleagues what they believe your strengths are. Sometimes, others see what you might overlook in yourself.

3. Structured assessments like the VIA Survey of Character Strengths or StrengthsFinder can highlight your unique qualities.

4. Compile a list of your strengths and talents. Include everything from interpersonal skills to creative abilities. Keep this list visible

as a reminder of what makes you special.

5. Now that you've identified your strengths, look for opportunities to develop and use them. Participate in activities that align with your skills to further boost your confidence and reinforce your identity.

Acknowledge your strengths as part of who you are; they empower you and build confidence in your individuality. Celebrating these unique qualities inspires positive self-reflection and motivation, which moves you forward on your journey of self-discovery.

Affirmations of Identity

Personal affirmations can celebrate your individuality and reinforce positive beliefs about yourself. Affirmations are reminders of your value and contributions; they help counteract societal pressures and unrealistic comparisons.

Create and use affirmations of identity:

1. Write a list of affirmations that resonate with you. Focus on aspects of yourself that you want to embrace, such as "I am worthy of love" or "My uniqueness is my strength."

2. Frame your affirmations in positive terms and avoid negative phrases. For instance, instead of saying, "I am not inadequate," say, "I am enough just as I am."

3. Make your affirmations personal to reflect your experiences and aspirations. The more personal they are, the more impactful

they'll be.

4. Recite your affirmations daily in front of a mirror, during meditation, or just vocalize them out loud whenever you are alone. The more you repeat them, the more you reinforce the beliefs you want to embody.

5. As you recite your affirmations, take a moment to visualize what it feels like to embody these affirmations. Picture yourself confidently embracing your individuality and strengths.

Affirmations cultivate a mindset that accepts and celebrates who you are. These empowering statements help dissolve self-doubt and reshape negative narratives, allowing you to value your individuality.

Surround Yourself with Positivity

Supportive environments and nurturing relationships can help to celebrate your individuality and improve your self-love. Positive surroundings validate and encourage you to be yourself.

Here are ways to create a positive atmosphere:

- Take stock of the environments you frequent, whether they be at home, work, or social settings. Are these spaces uplifting and supportive? Or do they make you miserable and weaken your self-image?

- Identify the people who celebrate your individuality. Think about friends and family who motivate you and appreciate your unique qualities. This could be in social circles, at work, or in your personal life.

- Join groups or organizations that celebrate diversity and inclusivity. You can also look for groups relevant to overcoming your past experiences. Being part of these communities nurtures a greater sense of self-acceptance and connection.

- Identify relationships or environments that diminish your self-worth or have a negative influence on your life. Set boundaries to protect yourself from negativity and surround yourself with positivity instead.

- Establish rituals that celebrate your individuality, such as hosting a gathering with supportive friends or dedicating time to activities that make you feel good.

Surround yourself with positivity to create a nurturing space that inspires you to embrace your uniqueness. Supportive relationships and environments can improve your self-acceptance and encourage you to pursue your authentic path.

Acknowledge Achievements

Reflecting on your past accomplishments makes it easier to celebrate your individuality and reinforce your identity. Your achievements—big or small—can help you cultivate a positive self-image and motivate you to pursue further goals, but only if you acknowledge how far you've come.

The following tips allow you to acknowledge your achievements:

- Start an accomplishment list where you record your successes, so that you can remind yourself of the good things you have done. Include achievements from various aspects of your life, such as personal milestones, career advancements, and creative projects.

- When reflecting on an accomplishment, think about the journey it took to get there. What challenges did you overcome? What did you learn about yourself? What are you proud of?

- Recognize and celebrate every victory. Each achievement is proof of your growth and abilities.

- Don't shy away from sharing your successes with others. Sharing can lead to encouragement and validation from your support network.

- Create a vision board to visualize your achievements and highlight your goals and successes. This can be an inspiring reminder of your unique journey and aspirations.

Recognizing and celebrating your achievements improves your self-love and appreciation for your individuality. Each accomplishment becomes a building block in reinforcing your identity, which empowers you to continue striving for your dreams and embrace who you are.

Let Go of Unrealistic Expectations

Expectations appear as beliefs or assumptions about how life should unfold and how people, including yourself, should behave. They can have a positive impact by providing motivation, direction, and a framework for setting goals. When used properly, expectations can inspire personal growth and achievement, which helps you strive for your best self.

However, when expectations become rigid or unrealistic, they can lead to disappointment and anxiety. Excessive pressure to meet external standards may decrease self-worth and create a fear of failure. Balancing healthy expectations with self-compassion is important to help you thrive with grace and authenticity.

Personal Expectations

You have to differentiate between personal goals and external expectations. While personal goals stem from your intrinsic desires and values, external expectations often arise from societal norms, family pressures, or cultural standards. Recognizing these external pressures can help you adopt a healthier approach to goal-setting.

Spend time identifying the difference:

1. Make a list of your current goals. Next to each goal, indicate whether it originates from your personal desires or from external pressures. This clarity helps you identify which goals resonate with you and which might be detrimental.

2. Think about sources of external expectations in your life. Are there societal norms, family beliefs, or peer influences that shape your aspirations? Write these down to help you recognize where these pressures come from, so that you can challenge them.

3. Once you've identified your personal goals and external expectations, reflect on your core values. Write down your top five values. Now, re-evaluate your goals to ensure they align with these values. Prioritize the goals that reflect your true self.

4. Place your goals somewhere you can see them regularly—like a sticky note on your mirror or set it as your phone background—to keep your mind focused on achieving them.

Identifying the distinction between expectations and goals allows you to, focus on representing your authentic self rather than conforming to unrealistic standards imposed by others. This shift creates a sense of self-acceptance and helps you pursue realistic goals that resonate with your identity.

Mindful Goal-Setting

Mindful goal-setting focuses on creating achievable objectives that reflect your authentic self and prioritize your values over societal pressures.

You can set personal goals using the following steps:

1. Identify what matters to you. What are your passions and desires? These ideas represent your core values.

2. Craft goals that honor these core values and ensure they align with your ideas of yourself.

3. Think about your future and how your core values and goals can help you develop a life plan that reflects your unique aspirations. Ensure you do not measure yourself through comparisons with others.

Setting realistic goals reduces feelings of inadequacy and anxiety, which helps create a sense of accomplishment that is based on personal growth and fulfillment. Every step you take in alignment with your true desires reinforces your self-worth and empowers you on your journey.

Release Perfectionism

Perfectionism can create an overwhelming pressure to meet unrealistic standards and hinder your ability to enjoy the process. Accept that imperfection is part of the human experience to help you learn and grow without fear of making mistakes.

Ways to develop a more forgiving mindset:

- Challenge the idea of perfection by identifying areas in your life where striving for perfection may be holding you back. Instead, focus on being "good enough." Doing your best is more than sufficient and allows for growth.

- When you make a mistake, view it as a learning opportunity and not a failure. Write down what you can learn from the experience instead of chastising yourself. It can make you more resilient and encourage you to view challenges from a growth perspective.

- Practicing gratitude can help release the need for perfectionism. Each day, write down three things you're grateful for, focusing on the progress you've made rather than what you didn't achieve. This practice shifts your mindset toward positivity and appreciation.

- Participate in creative activities without the pressure of perfection. It can be pottery, playing an instrument, or anything else that allows you to enjoy the process rather than fixating on the final product. The idea is to free yourself from rigid expectations and rekindle your sense of joy.

Perfectionism can slow down your progress, as it may cause unrealistic expectations. It's much better to be gentle with yourself and accept that small steps can move you forward.

Personal Mantras

Personal mantras are similar to affirmations and can help you let go of unrealistic expectations that may weigh you down. Mantras reinforce your commitment to your values and remind you to stay focused on what matters. A good mantra to start with is "I am who I am, love who I'm becoming, and embrace myself fully, flaws and all."

1. Use your core beliefs and values to create personal mantras that appeal to your identity or areas where you struggle with self-doubt. For example, if you often feel inadequate because of external expectations, consider a mantra around self-worth, such as "I am perfect just as I am and don't need external validation."

2. Phrase your mantras positively. Instead of saying, "I will not fail," reframe it as "Failure is okay because I can learn from all experiences." This shift develops a more empowering mindset.

3. Repeat your mantras with intention and allow them to sink into your consciousness.

4. Write your mantras on sticky notes and place them where you'll see them frequently, like on your bathroom mirror, computer, or refrigerator. These visual cues are constant reminders to embrace your uniqueness.

5. Recite your mantras when you are faced with self-doubt or exter-

nal pressures to help ground yourself and reaffirm your worth. It will increase your resilience and help you stay focused on personal values amidst the chaos.

Your mantras should resonate with your identity. Reciting these phrases strengthens your resolve against external pressures and helps ground you in authenticity. This encourages resilience and empowerment, reminding you that self-worth is inherent and does not depend on meeting the demands of others.

Key Takeaways

Unapologetic self-love is a journey where you continuously learn more about your identity. Each step you take towards authenticity strengthens your connection with yourself and reinforces your self-worth. Accepting who you truly are allows you to shed the weight of societal expectations and find freedom in expressing your individuality. It's okay to stumble along the way; growth often comes from embracing imperfections and learning from them. You'll find a renewed sense of courage to honor your true self along the way. Self-acceptance is an act of self-love, and with every step, you're reclaiming your joy and strengthening your emotional independence.

Chapter Three

Challenging Negative Thoughts

Negative thoughts can creep into our minds at any moment. You have to challenge them to move forward with self-love. This chapter offers you a safe space to confront those persistent doubts and harmful beliefs that hold you back. Recognizing the impact of negative thinking helps you to take control of your story and reshape your thoughts into empowering affirmations. With practical exercises and insightful guidance, you'll learn how to change your mindset and set yourself up for personal growth and resilience. Get ready to challenge the status quo and reclaim the joy that comes from a positive mindset.

Cognitive Restructuring Techniques for Self-Talk

Cognitive restructuring is a way to change negative thoughts into more positive ones. It's a helpful technique after experiencing trauma or difficult relationships since these events may have affected your self-perception. By learning to challenge and reframe your negative self-talk, you can build a healthier self-image. This process helps you let go of harmful beliefs that hold you back and empowers you to regain control over your thoughts and feelings. As you work on cognitive restructuring, you'll find it easier to heal emotionally and embrace who you are.

Identifying Automatic Thoughts

Changing your self-talk begins with recognizing the automatic thoughts that pop up in your daily life. These are the quick, negative thoughts that may arise without you even realizing it, often triggered by situations, interactions, or experiences. For instance, when you make a mistake, you might automatically think, "I always mess things up."

Discovering these automatic thoughts enables you to change them. Acknowledge that these thoughts are not always reflective of reality. They often come from past experiences or deep-seated beliefs that don't serve you anymore. Everyone experiences negative thoughts, and that knowledge can help you feel less alone in your struggles. It's a common human experience, and recognizing this can lessen feelings of isolation and self-doubt.

To conquer automatic thoughts:

1. Take a moment each day to notice the quick, negative thoughts that pop up. Use a notepad or your phone to jot them down as they come to you in real-life situations.

2. Label your negative thoughts when you catch them. For instance, if you think, "I always fail," write down "Automatic Thought: Self-Criticism." This helps create awareness.

3. Identify what triggered that negative thought. Did it occur after a conversation, a mistake, or a moment of self-reflection? Understanding the trigger helps in recognizing patterns.

4. Remind yourself that negative thoughts are common to everyone. Write affirmations such as, "I am not alone in feeling this way," to reinforce this idea.

Challenging Negative Beliefs

Once you've identified your automatic thoughts, the next step is to challenge the negative beliefs associated with them. Evaluating the evidence for and against these beliefs can lead to a more balanced perspective.

Ask yourself questions like:

- Is this thought based on facts or feelings?

- Is there evidence to support this thought?

- What would I say to a friend who thinks this way?

For example, if you believe "I am unlovable," think about the times when people have shown you love and support. Even something like smiling at you or giving you a hug is an indicator of care.

Remind yourself that beliefs can be altered. It can inspire confidence in your ability to pursue personal change and growth. Work on consciously replacing irrational thoughts with rational ones. Instead of thinking, "I'll never succeed," try shifting to, "I've faced challenges before, and I can handle this one too." This reinforces a positive mindset and helps you build resilience against negativity.

Spend some time countering your negative beliefs:

1. Write down the beliefs that emerge from your automatic

thoughts. Examples include "I am not clever" or "I'm not good enough."

2. For each belief, create two columns: "Supporting Evidence" and "Contradicting Evidence." Write down everything that supports your negative belief on one side and anything that contradicts it on the other.

3. Look at the contradictions and reframe your negative belief into something more balanced. For instance, change "I am not clever" to "I have learned a lot, and I am capable of improving my skills."

4. Replace negative beliefs with rational responses. For example, instead of thinking "I'll never succeed," tell yourself, "I have a track record of overcoming challenges and can succeed again."

5. Spend five minutes each day focusing on reframing one negative belief. Write the original thought, the evidence against it, and the new, constructive belief.

Create Affirmative Statements

Affirmations can be used to challenge the negative narratives you've been holding onto. They can help you develop a more supportive inner dialogue. Regularly repeating positive statements actively trains your mind to shift toward self-acceptance. This consistent practice can help build resilience against future negativity, allowing you to feel stronger and more capable of facing challenges as they arise. For example, if you often think, "I will never be happy," you can replace it with, "I am allowed to experience all emotions."

Make it a habit to create a list of affirmations that resonate with you. Choose statements that truly reflect your goals and values, and place them in visible areas where you can see them daily and internalize your worth. We discussed how to create affirmations in Chapter 1; review those steps if necessary.

For now, you can reflect and personalize this list of affirmations to overcome negative thoughts:

- I acknowledge my negative thoughts, but I choose to focus on the positive.

- Every challenge I face is an opportunity for growth and learning.

- I am capable of turning my doubts into strengths.

- I release the need to be perfect and embrace my authentic self.

- My past does not determine my future; I can change at any moment.

- I am worthy of love, success, and happiness.

- I choose to think positively and appreciate the good in my life.

Choose five affirmations and repeat them out loud each morning to make them part of your identity.

Thought Journals

A thought journal can be added to your daily routine for clarity and self-reflection. Documenting your thoughts and feelings allows you to differentiate between emotions and facts, which helps you think clearly. Set aside a few minutes each day to write down any automatic thoughts or negative beliefs that arise, and see if you can identify any patterns. Once you recognize these patterns, you can begin to deal with the recurring negative thoughts that may be holding you back.

Dedicate a specific time each day for journaling. You can use a physical notebook or a digital journaling app, whatever feels most comfortable for you.

Do the following:

1.

2. The thought you had

3. What triggered the thought

4. How you felt during that moment

5. After writing down your thoughts, identify which parts are emotions and which parts are factual. For instance, "I feel worthless" is an emotion, while "I received constructive criticism at work" is factual. Do you feel any different about the situation now that you've differentiated between fact and emotion?

6. Review your journal entries at the end of each week to identify patterns. Do certain triggers appear frequently? Are specific negative thoughts recurring? Summarize what you've learned about your thought patterns.

7. Based on your reflections, set goals for improving your thinking.

For example, if you often feel criticized by others, your goal could be to reframe feedback as an opportunity for growth rather than a personal attack.

Don't forget to revisit past journal entries and summaries regularly, such as every few weeks. This will show you how far you've come, how you have changed, and may also reveal areas for improvement. Patterns of negative thinking often become more apparent upon review, and this insight can guide your efforts in challenging and changing these thoughts. Change takes time, but with regular practice, you'll begin to notice the positive shifts in how you think and feel about yourself.

Mindfulness Strategies for Reducing Anxiety and Stress

Mindfulness is a tool to reduce anxiety and stress, particularly when these feelings stem from negative thoughts. Mindfulness encourages you to stay rooted in the present moment and allows you to become aware of your thoughts without being consumed by them. This awareness creates a buffer against constant anxious thinking and enables you to recognize that negative thoughts are just that—thoughts, not definitive truths.

When you practice mindfulness, you learn to observe your mental chatter with curiosity rather than judgment. This change in perspective can alleviate the weight of anxiety, helping you understand that these thoughts do not define your reality. Mindfulness helps you accept your feelings and allows you to acknowledge anxiety and stress without attempting to fight or escape them. This acceptance increases resilience and empowers you to tackle challenging emotions more easily, leading to a more balanced and peaceful state of mind.

Breathing Exercises

Breathing exercises can help you center your attention and calm your mind during moments of heightened anxiety. When you feel panic rising or negative thoughts creeping in, focusing on your breath can bring immediate relief.

The 4–7–8 breathing technique can be done anywhere:

1. Inhale deeply through your nose for four seconds.

2. Hold your breath for seven seconds.

3. Exhale slowly through your mouth for eight seconds.

4. Repeat this cycle several times.

The rhythmic nature of this breathing technique offers a grounding method that can help combat racing thoughts. With continued practice, breath control improves mindfulness and emotional regulation, allowing you to respond to negative thoughts more calmly and effectively.

Mindful Observation

Mindful observation teaches you to acknowledge your thoughts without judgment. Instead of trying to suppress or control your negative thoughts, you can learn to observe them as they arise.

Here's how:

1. When a negative thought pops up, pause for a moment and acknowledge its presence. Do not react immediately.

2. Simply notice that thought as it passes by, almost like when a cloud moves across the sky.

3. Let go of the thought and move on with the rest of your day.

Thoughts are transient, and realizing that can reduce their power over your emotional state. As you practice this technique, you develop a healthier relationship with your thoughts. You begin to understand that thoughts come and go, and they do not have to dictate how you feel or what actions you take. This distance helps you respond to negative self-talk with more objectivity and compassion.

Guided Visualization

Guided visualization is a technique that lets you imagine positive outcomes to counter feelings of anxiety. In times when you find yourself gripped by doubt or fear, take a moment to visualize a different scenario.

Picture yourself succeeding at a task, feeling confident, and experiencing joy:

1. Sit or lie down in a quiet and comfortable place where you won't be disturbed. Close your eyes and take a few deep breaths to relax your body.

2. Define the situation that is causing you stress or anxiety. Identify a positive outcome you wish to visualize, such as feeling calm, confident, or in control.

3. Picture the scenario in detail. Imagine yourself in the setting and observe it as if you're watching a movie. What does the positive

outcome look like? Focus on the sights, sounds, and feelings associated with the positive outcome.

4. Use all five senses to enhance your visualization. What do you see, hear, feel, smell, and taste in this positive scenario? The visualization should be vivid and realistic.

5. After thoroughly visualizing the positive outcome, take a moment to feel gratitude and joy for this visualization.

6. Slowly open your eyes, and carry the sense of calm and positivity with you as you face the day.

Envisioning success lifts your spirits and motivates you to take proactive actions in real life. This shift in focus from doubts to possibilities helps rewire your thought patterns. Regularly practicing guided visualization can train your mind to associate positive emotions with specific situations, reducing the grip of anxiety and enabling you to approach challenges with greater confidence.

Body Scan Meditation

Body scan meditation makes you more aware of physical sensations linked to your thoughts and emotions. Taking the time to pay attention to your body creates a stronger connection between your mind and physical sensations.

Do a body scan meditation when you have some time:

1. Find a quiet place to sit or lie down comfortably. Breathe deeply as you gently close your eyes.

2. Start at the top of your head and notice any areas of stress or tension.

3. Gradually move your focus down through your body: Neck, shoulders, arms, chest, abdomen, hips, buttocks, thighs, calves, and feet. Are you holding any tension in these areas?

4. Acknowledge these sensations and breathe into those areas, allowing relaxation to flow through your entire body.

Identifying stress points in your body can help you use targeted relaxation techniques. For instance, if you notice tension in your shoulders, practice releasing that tension by consciously relaxing the muscles and breathing deeply. Over time, this practice can help reduce anxiety and improve your ability to manage negative thoughts.

Breaking Free from Perfectionism

Perfectionism is closely linked to negative thoughts, as it creates a constant pressure to be flawless. When you only expect the best from yourself, any mistake or shortcoming can lead to harsh self-criticism and feelings of not being good enough. This mindset initiates a cycle of negative self-talk and convinces you that you must achieve perfection to be worthy or accepted. Fear of failure or judgment can become overwhelming, which stops you from trying new things or taking risks.

Redefining Success

You can overcome negative thoughts brought about by perfectionism by redefining success. It's important to realize that success is subjective to help alleviate feelings of inadequacy.

You can define success for yourself:

1. Take a moment to write down your core values, such as family, health, creativity, or personal growth. How do these values affect your perception of success?

2. Create a personal definition of success that resonates with you and reduces the pressure of societal expectations. For example, rather than striving for conventional success, you might define it as "feeling fulfilled in my daily activities" or "building supportive relationships."

3. Use your Achievements List from Chapter 2 and expand it to include your successes. Each week, write down at least three wins, like completing a task at work, helping a friend, or learning a new skill. These wins should align with your definition of success.

4. As you reflect on your successes, your mistakes might pop up too. Alter your perspective on mistakes by viewing them as opportunities to learn rather than reasons to criticize yourself. Create a list of past mistakes along with the valuable lessons you derived from each one. Can you identify success in how you overcame your mistakes?

Success is personal to you. Acknowledging these small victories builds confidence and counters negative self-talk by reinforcing your sense of accomplishment. When negative thoughts do pop up, refer back to this list to remind yourself that growth often comes from setbacks and that every misstep contributes to your growth. Continuously reflect on your successes and choose to move forward with positivity.

Set Realistic Goals

You can manage negative thoughts and stay motivated by setting realistic goals. In Chapter 2, you created mindful goals, but are they realistic? Perfectionism can lead to lofty goals that are tough to achieve. Review and adjust those foals now, then break them down into smaller, achievable steps.

For instance, if your goal is to practice mindfulness daily, write detailed action steps, such as:

1. **Week 1:** Do deep breathing exercises for three minutes a day, three times a week.

2. **Week 2:** Make the deep breathing exercise a daily practice.

3. **Week 3:** Include a body scan meditation with one deep breathing exercise every week.

Tracking your progress can reinforce positive thoughts and counteract feelings of perfectionism, as you can see your success. Use a planner or app to monitor your steps, and reward yourself for completing them. You should experience a sense of accomplishment that supports a positive mindset. Reassess your goals occasionally and adjust them to align with your evolving priorities and personal growth. This can reduce the likelihood of negative thoughts linked to underachievement.

Limiting Comparison

Comparison can lead to negative thoughts and trying to be perfect. You've already defined your personal goals based on your values and know why they are important to you. Choosing to focus on your aspirations can help you stay grounded rather than measuring your worth against others. This helps you develop a more positive mindset.

Here are some ways to reduce the comparisons:

- Reflect on the areas where you feel compelled to compare yourself to others. Write down the names of people you frequently compare yourself to, along with the attributes or achievements that trigger these feelings. Next, document three things that make your journey unique by focusing on your strengths and experiences.

- Create a "Gratitude Journal" to combat negative thoughts that stem from comparison. Each day, write down three elements of your life that you are grateful for, particularly those related to your growth. This practice moves your focus from what others are doing to appreciating your own experiences and accomplishments.

- Set boundaries with social media to limit your exposure to triggering content. Think about unfollowing accounts that evoke comparison, and replace them with uplifting, inspirational content instead. The idea is to curate a virtual space that increases positive thoughts and reduces feelings of inadequacy.

Developing Self-Acceptance

Self-acceptance helps with overcoming perfectionism and negative thoughts about yourself. You are good enough just as you are.

- Embracing your imperfections and realizing that they are part of being human. Make a list of your flaws, and next to each one, write a positive trait that balances it out. For example, if you consider yourself disorganized, you might acknowledge that you are also creative and adaptable.

- Practice self-compassion by speaking to yourself as you would to a friend. Every time you engage in negative self-talk, turn those thoughts into kind and understanding statements. Instead of thinking, "I always mess up," reframe it to, "I did my best, and I can improve next time." This perspective change can help mitigate feelings of inadequacy and ease negative thoughts.

- Participate in activities that increase your self-love, such as writing a letter to yourself expressing gratitude for your unique qualities and experiences. Revisit this letter during tough times to remind yourself of your worth and the journey you're on.

- Continue to use daily affirmations that focus on self-acceptance. For example, "I am worthy of love" or "I embrace my imperfections." Recite these affirmations daily to reinforce positive self-perception and reduce negative thoughts.

Key Takeaways

Negative thoughts will pop up as you work on loving yourself, but you can overcome them. The process of self-love is ongoing, and each step you take to redefine your thoughts contributes to a healthier mindset and a more fulfilling life. By consciously applying the techniques in this chapter, you enable yourself to rise above self-doubt and embrace your true self with confidence. Carry every small victory with you as you continue to tackle life's challenges and remember that you possess the power to redefine your thoughts and, in turn, your reality.

Chapter Four

Building Self-Compassion

It's easy to criticize and judge yourself, which makes having self-compassion feel like an act of rebellion. But this is the most heartfelt gift you can offer yourself. In this chapter, you will learn how to embrace kindness and acceptance so that your internal dialogue changes from harsh criticism to understanding and support. Self-compassion does not overlook your flaws, but it requires acknowledging them with an open heart that allows grace to replace guilt. The focus becomes encouragement instead of judgment, and forgiveness instead of lingering regret.

The Power of Self-Kindness

Self-kindness means treating yourself with compassion and understanding, similar to how you would extend kindness to others. It involves acknowledging your suffering and responding with warmth, care, and empathy, rather than harsh criticism and judgment. Self-kindness encourages you to accept your imperfections and recognize that everyone experiences difficulties and makes mistakes. Choosing to speak to yourself in a gentle and supportive manner nurtures an inner dialogue that leads to emotional resilience and healing. Self-kindness empowers you to acknowledge your worth, improve your well-being, and develop a deeper connection with yourself on the journey to self-love.

Self-Kindness vs. Self-Judgment

The difference between self-kindness and self-judgment affects emotional well-being. While self-judgment may seem rational, it often results in feelings of shame and inadequacy. Judging yourself harshly creates a cycle of negativity that slows down healing. In contrast, self-kindness offers a nurturing response to your struggles. It allows you to embrace your flaws and mistakes with compassion rather than condemnation.

Self-kindness helps with emotional recovery, decreases negative self-talk, and nurtures a healthier self-image. Imagine speaking to yourself with words of encouragement instead of criticism. This change in perspective can have a positive impact on your mental health. Self-kindness also encourages patience as you experience personal growth. Instead of demanding immediate results, you learn to appreciate the process, allowing for gradual, sustainable change.

The Science Behind Self-Compassion

Self-compassion increases your resilience, which helps you bounce back from setbacks more easily. Even when you face challenges, self-kindness makes it more likely that you will view difficulties as opportunities for growth rather than insurmountable obstacles. Self-compassion has been linked to lower levels of anxiety and depression (Gillette, 2024). You create a safe space for emotional expression and healing when you adopt a gentle approach to your feelings. This supportive mindset stimulates emotional stability, enabling you to handle life's ups and downs with greater ease.

Self-kindness can also strengthen your motivation (Perry, 2022). An environment where failure is seen as a natural part of growth makes it more likely for you to pursue your goals without fear. This mindset change allows you to welcome challenges and engage fully in personal development without the weight of self-criticism.

Everyday Tips for Self-Kindness

There are various ways to incorporate self-kindness into your daily life. The more you practice being kind to yourself, the easier it will become.

Some tips to help you practice self-kindness:

- Practice small acts of kindness: Start with simple gestures that reflect kindness towards yourself. This could be taking a moment to appreciate your efforts, complimenting yourself, or treating yourself to something you enjoy. Small actions can alter your perspective over time.

- Create dedicated moments in your day for self-kindness. It could include journaling, meditating, or taking a walk. These rituals promote self-kindness and reinforce a positive mindset.

- Make self-care a priority in your routine. You can replenish your emotional reserves by enjoying a relaxing bath, reading a favorite book, or spending time with loved ones. You deserve the same care and attention that you extend to others.

- Identify situations or people that contribute to negative self-talk and set boundaries to limit their influence. Boundaries can create a healthier environment that nurtures self-kindness and allows you to focus on positive growth.

Debunking the Myths of Self-Kindness

Despite its many benefits, self-kindness is often misunderstood. A common myth is that self-kindness is the same as self-indulgence or weakness. In reality, self-kindness is a strength that builds resilience and personal growth because you are recognizing your worth and acknowledging your struggles without judgment. Another misconception is that being kind to yourself means avoiding accountability. On the contrary, self-kindness encourages you to advocate for yourself. It allows you to take responsibility for your actions while approaching your shortcomings with compassion. This balance between self-advocacy and self-care helps with personal development.

Do not allow yourself to be held back by these myths. Releasing them frees you from the constraints of societal expectations and empowers you to have a kinder relationship with yourself.

Increase Your Self-Acceptance

Self-acceptance, self-compassion, and self-kindness occur when you focus on internal validation and emotional growth. The idea is to know yourself better and turn negative thought patterns into uplifting affirmations. You can nurture a supportive inner dialogue that boosts healing and resilience with the exercises in this section.

Mirror Work

Mirror work uses a combination of self-affirmations and personal observation to create positive self-acknowledgment and reduce self-criticism. Standing in front of a mirror and speaking affirmations aloud creates a direct connection between your words and your self-image.

Use these steps for mirror work:

1. Stand in front of a mirror where you feel comfortable and can see your entire reflection.

2. Spend a few minutes breathing deeply to center yourself. Set a clear intention for the practice, such as nurturing self-love or acceptance.

3. Say positive affirmations out loud, such as "I am worthy of love" or "I embrace my unique qualities." You can use the affirmations you created in previous chapters. Speak these words with conviction and sincerity.

4. Pay attention to your feelings and thoughts as you say your affirmations. Notice any discomfort or resistance that may pop up. Look at your body and see if you can identify any areas that seem tense as you say these words.

5. Repeat the mirror work exercise regularly, ideally daily or a few times a week. Over time, you'll notice an improvement in your self-perception and self-acceptance.

With repeated practice, you can reinforce self-acceptance over time. This can change your perception of your physical and emotional flaws and turn them into sources of strength and resilience.

Expressing Thoughts and Feelings

Journaling—through writing, typing, recording, or in any other form—helps you recognize negative patterns and track your progress in self-acceptance as time goes by. It's a safe space for expressing vulnerability and processing emotions without judgment. You can clarify your self-perceptions and identify areas of struggle more clearly.

Express your thoughts and feelings:

1. Allocate a specific time daily or weekly for journaling. Consistency improves its effectiveness.

2. Use prompts like:

3.

4. What do I love about myself today?

5. What challenges have I faced, and how have I overcome them?

6. What qualities do I want to embrace more fully?

7. Express yourself without self-editing or worrying about grammar. Let your thoughts flow freely.

8. Revisit your expressions occasionally to track your progress and identify growth. Acknowledge how your perception of yourself

has evolved over time.

Guided Meditation for Inner Acceptance

Mindfulness through guided meditation can help you develop self-acceptance in a gentle and nurturing way. This practice uses breathing techniques to relax your body and mind while focusing on self-worth. Guided meditation creates a compassionate inner dialogue and encourages you to treat yourself with kindness and understanding. This mindful space allows you to acknowledge and process emotions without judgment, which enables deeper self-reflection.

The following steps will guide you through the meditation:

1. Choose a quiet spot where you won't be disturbed and sit or lie down comfortably.

2. Decide how long you'd like to meditate—start with 5-10 minutes and gradually increase the time as you become more comfortable.

3. Close your eyes and take a few deep breaths, inhaling slowly through your nose and exhaling through your mouth.

4. Visualize a warm light radiating from your heart. As you breathe, picture this light growing brighter and enveloping you in warmth and acceptance.

5. During the meditation, repeat phrases such as "May I be kind to myself" or "I accept myself as I am." Allow these affirmations to resonate within you.

6. If any emotions arise, acknowledge them without judgment. Just

sit with these feelings, observe them, and breathe through them.

7. When your timer goes off, take a few deep breaths, slowly open your eyes, and take a moment to reflect on your experience.

Gratitude Exercises

Gratitude encourages you to reflect on your personal qualities and strengths, resulting in a consistent focus on positive attributes. It moves your mindset away from self-criticism and helps you appreciate yourself. Regularly acknowledging what you value about yourself strengthens the connection you have with your self-worth and values.

Practice gratitude by reflecting on the following questions at the end of each day or week:

- What are three qualities I appreciate about myself today?

- What accomplishments am I proud of this week?

- Who in my life brings out my positive attributes, and how do they influence me?

- What do other people appreciate or love about me?

- What do I have to be thankful for now that I didn't have a week, month, or year ago?

Record your responses in a way that works for you. Focus on small and significant traits or accomplishments, allowing yourself to feel appreciation for your life. Use your gratitude reflections as reminders of your strengths and to reinforce a positive self-image and self-acceptance.

Rewriting Your Internal Dialogue

You are the only one who can write and rewrite your story. It's a transformative experience that empowers you to reshape your reality. Consciously choosing to speak to yourself with kindness and encouragement creates a more supportive internal environment that improves your self-esteem and emotional resilience, helping you handle challenges more easily. Positive self-talk can alleviate stress and anxiety by replacing negative thoughts with uplifting affirmations that reinforce your worth and capabilities (Zoppi, 2024). An optimistic inner voice sets the stage for personal growth and a deeper connection with your true self, which sets you up for unapologetic self-love.

Identifying Harmful Patterns

Rewriting your internal dialogue starts with identifying negative narratives that may cloud your self-perception. This process requires self-awareness, which is the ability to observe your thoughts without judgment. Take a moment to tune into your internal monologue. What do you frequently tell yourself during challenging moments? Is there a consistent theme of criticism or doubt? These harmful patterns can be rooted in past experiences, societal pressure, or even comparing yourself to others.

These negative ideas about yourself require constructive cognitive restructuring, which was discussed in the previous chapter. Confronting your internal dialogue creates an opportunity to understand the emotional triggers that drive your negative thoughts. Are these thoughts rooted in fear, past failures, or societal standards? Think carefully about the origins of these critical voices, so that you can begin to challenge their validity.

Awareness is the key to dismantling the grip of negative self-talk and developing a more compassionate internal narrative.

Creating Positive Counter-Narratives

Now that you've become aware of your negative thoughts, it's time to develop positive counter-narratives that challenge these harmful ideas. Once again, affirmations that reflect your worth and capabilities are useful. For example, if you often think, "I will never have a good life," turn it into, "I am worthy of happiness and fulfilment." These affirmations reshape your thoughts and give you a more balanced perspective on your abilities.

Be proactive with this transformation by consistently using these affirmations during your daily routine. Write them down, save them on your phone, say them aloud, and visualize their truth. Over time, these positive statements will become embedded in your mind and gradually replace the negative self-talk that once held power over you. Creating an environment of self-acceptance gives you a nurturing space where positivity can flourish. It allows your self-perception to become more empowering and compassionate.

The Power of Repetition

Changing your internal dialogue requires consistent practice and repetition. Just like any skill, changing negative thought patterns into positive affirmations takes time and dedication. Find moments in your day—perhaps during morning routines, as you have your lunch break, in the car, or before bedtime—to dedicate to your affirmations. Repeat them as much as possible.

But keep in mind that setbacks may occur along the way. They are part of the learning process and do not signify failure. Mistakes are perfectly normal. Be gentle with yourself during these moments, and accept that changing your thought patterns is an ongoing process. The key is to reinforce your commitment to self-love and acceptance through continued practice, even when challenges arise. Each time you choose a positive thought over a negative one, you take another step toward a more compassionate inner dialogue.

Support Systems and Changing Your Story

As you rewrite your internal dialogue, turn to supportive individuals who can help you. Surrounding yourself with uplifting and encouraging people creates a framework for reinforcing positive ideas. Their feedback can provide valuable insights and affirmations that boost your self-image.

When you share your struggles with trusted friends or family members, they can validate your experiences and motivate you to overcome internal barriers. Your support system should understand your past, the path you are on, and your aspirations. You can join a support group, participate in workshops, or connect with a therapist to share your experiences, build resilience, and instill a sense of community.

Sharing your dreams and affirmations with others can also make the practice feel more tangible. Your support system can encourage you and remind you of your worth and potential, which empowers you to challenge negative self-talk more effectively. As a result, you reinforce your commitment to self-love and self-acceptance.

Key Takeaways

Developing self-kindness and acceptance is an ongoing process. Self-compassion allows you to treat yourself with the love and understanding you inherently deserve. You have the ability to reframe your internal narrative and the choice to respond with warmth instead of criticism. This creates a nurturing environment for healing and growth, where each step you take towards self-compassion brings you closer to a more authentic and joyful life, free from the weight of self-doubt. Setbacks will happen, but they do not define you. Commit to being your own ally, honoring your feelings, and celebrating your progress. You will find empowerment in vulnerability and strength in your heart, which allows unapologetic self-love to flourish in every aspect of your life.

Chapter Five

Letting Go of Past Hurts

The past hurts, but you have to let go of it to move forward with self-love and personal growth. It's all too easy to become entangled in the pain of former experiences, allowing them to affect how you see yourself and interact with the world. These experiences have contributed to who you are, but they do not have to have a hold on your future. You can reframe your past and view it as a collection of lessons rather than burdens to liberate yourself from guilt, resentment, and self-doubt. In this chapter, you will discover strategies to release the emotional weight of past hurts, empowering you to embrace your identity and reclaim your joy.

Healing From Past Experiences and Emotional Wounds

Recognizing your emotional wounds is necessary for healing and self-discovery. The pain you've gone through can give you insight into how it influences your thoughts, feelings, and actions. You allow yourself to grow and transform when you confront these wounds. Identifying the root of your emotions can uncover patterns that have held you back and give you the power to release those limitations. This process helps with healing and sets you up to become a stronger, more resilient version of yourself.

Identifying Emotional Wounds

Emotional wounds are often rooted in past experiences and may have an impact on your mental, emotional, and physical well-being. Symptoms of unresolved emotional trauma can appear as anxiety, depression, irritability, or feelings of hopelessness (Gupta, 2023). You can recognize the signs of these wounds by paying attention to your behavioral patterns. They can shed light on deeper issues caused by unresolved wounds.

Look for the following signs:

- **Avoidance:** You might find yourself avoiding certain situations or people that remind you of painful experiences.

- **Emotional Outbursts:** Small triggers can lead to intense emotional reactions, which indicate buried feelings.

- **Perfectionism:** An overwhelming desire to be perfect often comes from fear of failure tied to past criticisms or traumas.

- **Difficulty in Relationships:** Struggling to have healthy relationships may signal unresolved issues affecting your ability to connect with others.

- **Negative Self-Talk:** Persistent feelings of worthlessness or self-doubt indicate that past experiences affect your current self-perception.

Acknowledge these patterns to better understand the impact of your emotional wounds.

Connecting Emotions to Experiences

Your emotional responses today can also be based on your past experiences. This connection helps to uncover the roots of your feelings. For instance, childhood experiences frequently affect how you handle adult relationships today. If you faced emotional neglect as a child, you might find trust and intimacy challenging as an adult.

Introspection

Introspection can help you understand your emotional triggers. Take time to reflect on moments when you reacted strongly.

Ask yourself:

- What was the situation?

- How did I feel?

- What thoughts were running through my mind at that moment?

- Did anything from my past pop up during this time?

This practice can reveal patterns and help you connect your emotional responses to past experiences.

Journaling to Process Emotions

Process your emotions using these prompts while journaling:

1. Describe a recent emotional reaction. What triggered it?

2. Write about a past experience that still affects you today.

3. List ways your childhood may influence your current behavior in relationships.

4. Reflect on your thoughts about self-worth. Where do these beliefs come from?

5. Identify a specific emotion you have trouble expressing. Explore why that is.

Journaling regularly can help develop greater emotional awareness and give insights into your healing.

Action Plan for Addressing Emotional Wounds

Confronting emotional pain is the only way you will heal. It might be uncomfortable and painful, but you have to work through these experiences if you want to move forward. An action plan can help you process these situations and how they affect your life. It comes down to confronting your pain, choosing healing methods, and being patient.

Confronting Emotional Pain

Your feelings are valid and worthy of attention. Take time to journal about your past experiences in any form like typing, painting, or talking,.

Here are the steps to guide you along the way:

1. Acknowledge and accept your emotions as valid, no matter how difficult they may be.

2. Record your thoughts, feelings, and experiences in your journal or other format to clarify what needs healing.

3. If you want to, you can confide in a trusted friend or family member to lighten your emotional load. However, a therapist can guide you in what to do with your emotions and help you heal faster.

4. If you feel overwhelmed, don't hesitate to reach out to a trained therapist or counselor who can provide personalized support and guidance.

Healing Modalities

Each of us heals in our own unique way. You can explore a variety of options to help you recover from past wounds, enabling you to live a fuller life.

Some healing modalities that may resonate with you:

- **Therapy:** Work with a mental health professional to explore your past and develop coping strategies. Look specifically for someone trained in trauma and healing practices, as they can help you work through your past and equip you for the future by using talk therapy or cognitive restructuring techniques.

- **Meditation:** Mindfulness and meditation can help you develop self-awareness and encourage emotional healing. It's ideal if you need to sit with your emotions in a non-judgmental way.

- **Yoga:** Yoga can connect your mind and body, which reduces stress and promotes healing. It's a great healing modality if you tend to process your emotions or daily events through movement.

- **Support groups**: Meeting with others who have experienced similar situations to your own can create a nurturing environment for processing emotions. These groups can offer valuable advice and a sense of community.

Practicing Patience

Healing from emotional wounds requires lots of patience. There will be ups and downs, and progress may come slowly, but each step you take is worth it. As you love yourself, focus on small, manageable actions that can lead to healing. Set realistic goals for yourself, like practicing gratitude a few times a week, getting support from friends, and not allowing yourself to speak negatively about yourself.

Acknowledge every step you take, regardless of how insignificant it may seem. Each moment of introspection, every session in therapy, and all progress made in your healing journey are worth celebrating. Your ongoing growth can increase your motivation and help you move forward.

The Role of Forgiveness in Self-Liberation

Forgiveness can give you emotional freedom and personal empowerment. When you hold onto grudges, you carry the weight of past hurts and allow them to dictate your emotions and thoughts. By choosing to forgive—whether it's yourself or others—you release that burden and reclaim your power. This act doesn't mean you condone the behavior that hurt you; rather, it signifies your decision to prioritize your well-being. Forgiveness opens your heart and creates space for healing and new possibilities. As you let go of anger, resentment, and blame, you create room for peace and happiness, which empowers you to continue with renewed strength and hope.

Carrying negative emotions can weigh you down and impact your mental and emotional well-being. You reclaim your personal power when you forgive and step away from the role of a victim. This shift allows you to focus on your growth and future rather than being anchored by past pains. Forgiveness enables you to take control of your story and directs your energy toward positive change.

The Process of Forgiveness

Forgiving yourself and others is a process.

Use these steps as a guide to forgiveness:

1. Start by recognizing your emotions, such as anger, pain, or betrayal. These feelings are essential to your healing process, as it helps you understand the situation and yourself better. Allow yourself to feel them without judgment.

2. Understand that forgiveness is not an obligation; it's a choice you make for your well-being. Decide consciously that you want to forgive and sit with that idea for some time. Forgiveness doesn't happen overnight and may require time and reflection.

3. Be gentle with yourself as you go through the process of forgiveness. Healing takes time and requires self-compassion. It's okay to struggle. Practice self-care and kindness as you process your

emotions, knowing that you deserve compassion.

4. Find a safe way to express what you're feeling using some of the ways we have spoken about, like journaling and talking to a trusted friend or counselor. You can also write a letter to the person who hurt you, regardless of whether you send it or not.

5. Remind yourself of the benefits of forgiveness, like the emotional freedom and peace that it can bring. Visualization can help: Imagine yourself letting go of the pain and embracing the lightness that comes with release.

6. This key moment in the process is choosing to let go. Make a conscious decision to release the resentment. You don't have to forget the past, but you can choose not to let it control your present.

Forgiveness as a Tool for Growth

Forgiveness can change you. It allows you to shed the negative emotional burdens that have held you back. You may experience growth in various areas of your life after forgiving yourself and others. Forgiveness releases emotional burdens when you cut the ties that bind you to past pain. This release is like lifting a heavy weight off your shoulders, bringing a sense of relief and lightness. In turn, you will experience healthier interactions with others. This newfound emotional space allows you to engage with others more openly and authentically, which develops trust and connection.

Forgiveness also builds resilience and increases your ability to handle future challenges. It strengthens your emotional toolkit and equips you to confront obstacles with a positive outlook. Letting go of anger opens your heart to joy. With a lighter emotional load, you adopt a more optimistic perspective and see opportunities for growth and happiness where once there was only pain.

Common Misconceptions About Forgiveness

As with many other things, there are some myths about forgiveness. It helps to be aware of them so that you don't accidentally slow down your progress.

Here are a few common misconceptions:

- **Forgiveness Means Forgetting:** Many people believe that to forgive, you must forget the wrongdoing. This isn't true. Forgiveness is about acknowledging the hurt while choosing not to let it affect you negatively in the future.

- **Forgiveness Means Excusing Behavior:** Just because you forgive someone doesn't mean you endorse their actions or excuse their behavior. It's possible to hold people accountable while still moving forward with your life.

- **Forgiveness Requires Reconciliation:** Some people think forgiving someone means reconciling with them. However, you can forgive without having a relationship with the person who hurt you. It's about freeing your heart, not necessarily re-establishing connections.

- **Forgiveness Is a Weakness:** There's a common perception that forgiveness is a sign of weakness. In reality, it takes immense strength and courage to forgive. Choosing to let go of anger reflects a deep commitment to your emotional well-being.

Understanding these misconceptions allows you to approach forgiveness with clarity and intent, which empowers you to make choices that will improve your emotional freedom and personal growth. The ability to forgive can lead to a life filled with joy, resilience, and healthier relationships.

Releasing Self-Blame and Guilt

Self-blame and guilt are normal when you are held back by the weight of past mistakes. It hinders your ability to move forward and embrace the present. But you know what? Everyone makes mistakes; you are not alone in your struggles. Constantly blaming yourself for past mistakes traps you in a negative cycle that perpetuates feelings of shame and guilt. This cycle can trap you in a mindset of victimhood, where you feel powerless and unable to break free.

Self-blame frequently comes from unrealistic expectations and societal pressures to perform flawlessly. The harsh judgments we place on ourselves can be influenced by external opinions and unattainable standards. However, acknowledging your imperfections allows you to practice self-compassion, creating space for healing. When you free yourself from the grip of self-blame and guilt, you can focus on learning and growth rather than dwelling on the past.

Challenging Negative Narratives

Countering self-blame and negative thoughts requires a proactive approach. You have to actively work on thinking differently.

Here are some techniques to help change your mindset:

- Reflect on past experiences and identify positive outcomes or growth that came from them. Focusing on the silver linings helps you to reframe your narrative, and you start to see mistakes as opportunities for learning rather than failures.

- Develop a more balanced view of your self-worth, one that is is not defined by your mistakes. Your strengths, accomplishments, and the value you bring to the world all form your self-worth, and a balanced perspective allows you to appreciate the entirety of who you are.

- Remember that everyone makes mistakes; it's simply part of being human. When you acknowledge that others also experience setbacks, it becomes easier to give yourself grace and compassion.

- Practice identifying negative thoughts as they arise and replacing them with more constructive and compassionate alternatives. For instance, instead of thinking, "I always mess things up," try reframing it as, "I made a mistake, but I can learn from it."

- Avoid comparing yourself to others, especially on social media. People often project curated versions of their lives and hide what is actually happening. Focus on your life instead.

Practicing Self-Forgiveness

Forgiving yourself for past actions can help you heal. It may seem impossible at the moment, but you are capable of forgiving and loving yourself.

The following steps guide the process of self-forgiveness:

1. Start by showing compassion to yourself. Think about it as treating yourself as you would a dear friend. Speak kindly to yourself and acknowledge your feelings while offering understanding and compassion. This practice helps dispel harsh self-judgment.

2. Spend time reflecting on the experiences you regret. What lessons did they teach you? How can they inform your choices moving forward? The positive insights from challenges can impact your growth and resilience.

3. Change your focus from guilt to growth. Rewrite your narrative to center around the person you are becoming as a result of your experiences. This new story emphasizes your resilience and commitment to self-improvement.

4. Set realistic intentions for the future based on your reflections. Focus on how you can apply what you've learned to initiate positive change in your life.

5. Be patient. Self-forgiveness is a continuous process, so allow yourself the time and space to heal without rushing.

Building a Supportive Environment

Your environment affects your healing, but with the right support, you can diminish self-blame.

Tips for creating a supportive atmosphere:

- Look for supportive groups or communities that have open discussions about personal struggles and emotional healing. Being around others who share their vulnerabilities can give you a sense of belonging and understanding.

- Identify friends, family, or mentors who inspire and uplift you. Positive influences can help reshape your perceptions and become reminders of your worth and potential.

- Have open conversations about mental health and emotional well-being within your social circles. Sharing your experiences and hearing others' stories reduces the stigma around self-blame and guilt, which helps everyone involved to heal.

- Be mindful of relationships or environments that result in judgment or criticism. Distance yourself from toxic situations that increase self-blame, and instead, surround yourself with people who nurture your growth and self-acceptance.

- Acknowledge the importance of supportive family, friends, and mentors, specifically those who offer encouragement and understanding during difficult times. Strengthening these bonds can help you heal and allow you to feel more supported in confronting self-blame.

Key Takeaways

Spend a few moments reflecting on the transformative process you've undertaken. Healing is not a linear process and requires a plan to make it effective. The act of forgiving yourself for past mistakes can liberate you, and as you release the burdens of self-blame and guilt, you start to reclaim your power and redefine your narrative. Every step you take is proof of your strength and resilience. Embrace the lessons learned from your past, but do not allow them to dictate your future. As you move forward, carry with you the knowledge that letting go opens the door to new opportunities for growth and joy. Trust in your ability to thrive, and know that each moment you choose to release gets you a step closer to your authentic self.

Chapter Six

Positive Relationships

Relationships are all around us, and they play a role in your emotions. Healthy connections can be a mirror that reflects our worth and reinforces our growth. This chapter explores the significance of nurturing positive relationships that uplift and inspire. As you learn to identify the qualities that define supportive connections, you will discover how they can increase your self-appreciation and reinforce your emotional independence. Other people become a sanctuary where self-love flourishes. There is power in community; it's time to tap into it.

Setting Healthy Boundaries Without Guilt

Boundaries are important for nurturing self-love and maintaining healthy relationships. Many of us have experienced moments when our boundaries were crossed, leading to feelings of frustration, resentment, or self-doubt. Think back to those times when you felt overwhelmed or disregarded; those experiences shaped your understanding of what you need to feel safe and valued. Setting boundaries is not selfish; it's an act of self-care that empowers you to protect your emotional well-being. Moving forward, you can create a future where your boundaries are respected.

Boundaries Matter

Boundaries are the invisible lines that define what is acceptable and what is not in our relationships. They are guidelines that help protect your emotional health and well-being. Healthy boundaries allow you to express your needs clearly, developing a sense of safety and respect. A well-defined boundary may include how much time you're willing to spend with others, the topics of conversation you're comfortable with, or behavior that you find unacceptable.

When boundaries are respected, they create an environment where you can thrive. The presence of clear boundaries can reduce anxiety and stress, which helps you feel more in control of your interactions. It's your right to handle relationships in a way that honors your sense of self.

The Importance of Saying No

Learning to say no when necessary is part of self-care. Saying no helps you to protect your time and energy, ensuring that you can allocate your resources to what matters to you. It also results in respect from others when they recognize your limits. When you assertively say no, you signal to others that you value your own needs and priorities, encouraging them to do the same.

Saying no takes practice, and it's best to start small. If someone invites you to an event that doesn't align with your interests or well-being, politely decline. You might say something like, "I appreciate the invitation, but I need some time to recharge." This practice builds your confidence and allows others to understand where your boundaries lie. It's important to remember that self-prioritization is not selfish; it's a necessary step toward living authentically and improving your emotional health.

Communicate Your Boundaries

Effective communication is the cornerstone of establishing boundaries. Clear communication can prevent misunderstandings and resentment that may occur when boundaries are not explained to others. Start by identifying which boundaries matter most to you and practice expressing them with honesty and clarity. For example, if you need quiet time after work, you could say, "I need some time to unwind after my day, so I won't be available to talk until later."

You set a tone of honesty in your relationships when you express boundaries directly. It's a way of saying, "I respect myself, and I hope you will respect me as well." Healthy discussions about boundaries result in mutual respect and understanding. Others will also be more inclined to share their boundaries because you are creating a safe space for open dialogue that enriches the connection between you and other people.

Overcoming Guilt

It's common to feel guilty for putting your needs first, but recognizing that boundaries are necessary for your well-being can help ease this guilt. Healthy relationships are those in which both individuals honor each other's needs. Your desires and limits are just as valid as anyone else's.

Practice self-compassion to overcome feelings of guilt. Acknowledge that what you are doing is protective and beneficial for yourself while creating healthier dynamics in your relationships. Remind yourself that just as you have needs, so do others, and setting boundaries does not diminish anyone else's worth or value. Each person's needs are valid and worth honoring, including yours. Begin by reframing how you perceive boundaries. Instead of seeing them as barriers to connection, view them as an essential part of authentic relationships.

How to Set Boundaries

Setting and implementing boundaries is easier said than done. With a plan and practice, you can make them work for you.

1. Spend some time reflecting on what you are comfortable with and where you feel your limits are being pushed. Think about different areas of your life, such as time, energy, and emotional availability. Write down some boundaries or non-negotiables based on this reflection.

2. State your boundaries as specifically as possible. Instead of saying, "I need space," clarify what that means: "I need some time alone on Wednesdays to recharge."

3. Frame your boundaries using "I" statements to express how you feel without sounding accusatory. For instance, "I feel overwhelmed when plans change last minute, and I need some time to adjust."

4. Approach boundary-setting with confidence. Practice assertive body language: stand tall, make eye contact, and speak clearly. If you're nervous, rehearse what you want to say ahead of time.

5. Expect that not everyone will respond positively to your bound-

aries initially. Be prepared for pushback and stay firm in your choices without feeling the need to justify yourself excessively.

6. Boundaries can evolve, so you need to reassess and adjust. Evaluate and revise your boundaries as needed to reflect your changing needs and circumstances.

7. If you struggle with setting or maintaining boundaries, get support from friends, mentors, or a therapist. They can provide perspectives and strategies to help you overcome these challenges.

Boundaries help you nurture self-love. They enable you to establish and communicate your limits without guilt, which creates space for genuine connections that honor who you are and support your emotional independence.

Identifying Toxic Relationships and Building a Support System

Not all connections serve your growth; some may drain your energy or undermine your sense of worth. These toxic relationships need to be replaced with relationships that contribute positively to a supportive environment that enables self-acceptance and joy. Healthy relationships uplift you, encourage personal growth, and reinforce your boundaries. Recognizing toxic dynamics allows you to make informed choices about who you surround yourself with, prioritizing relationships that celebrate your worth.

Signs of Toxic Relationships

Identifying signs of unhealthy relationships helps to safeguard your emotional health and develop self-love. Toxic relationships can drain your emotional energy and lead to feelings of exhaustion, anxiety, and diminished self-esteem (Foy, 2023). To recognize these unhealthy dynamics, pay close attention to how you feel before, during, and after interacting with certain individuals. Are you consistently feeling depleted after spending time with them? Do you notice any patterns of behavior that leave you feeling bad about yourself? These are red flags that suggest you may be stuck in a toxic relationship.

Signs of toxicity can appear in various ways:

- You may notice excessive criticism, manipulation, or a lack of support.

- The other person may belittle your achievements, disregard your feelings, or impose their views without considering yours.

- Your instincts scream for you to withdraw from the person.

- Your happiness hinges on their approval.

Being aware of these signs helps you avoid further emotional damage and empowers you to make informed choices about the relationships you nurture in your life.

Characteristics of Supportive Relationships

On the other hand, supportive relationships can guide your social choices. Supportive connections encourage your growth and give a sense of belonging. They create a nurturing environment where you feel safe to be yourself without fear of judgment or criticism.

Genuine relationships have specific characteristics:

- They provide empathy and understanding freely, which allows you to share your thoughts and struggles without hesitation.

- You feel uplifted after conversations rather than drained.

- You experience personal growth and exploration without resorting to competition or harmful comparisons.

- The other person celebrates your successes and encourages you as you take steps toward your goals, rather than viewing them as threats.

- Supportive individuals are willing to listen and engage in meaningful conversation; they value what you have to say.

- They maintain open lines of communication and create space for vulnerability, allowing both of you to share your experiences honestly.

Can you identify these kinds of relationships in your life? Evaluate your connections, and look for friends or mentors who demonstrate compassion, patience, and trustworthiness. These characteristics form the foundation for relationships that support you and encourage a deeper understanding of your self-worth.

Evaluate Current Relationships

Now that you understand the signs of toxicity and the traits of supportive relationships, take the time to reflect on your existing connections. Evaluating your relationships helps to uncover which ones contribute to your well-being and cultivate your self-love.

Think about the following:

1. Assess the balance of give and take in each relationship. Do you feel valued, heard, and appreciated, or do you often find yourself compromising your needs for the sake of others?

2. Reflect in your preferred way, such as journaling your feelings, discussing your thoughts with a trusted friend, or meditating on your interactions. Think about the emotional impact of each relationship to reveal patterns you may not have noticed before.

3. After considering how your connections affect you, make a list of relationships that consistently uplift you and those that drain your energy. Identify individuals who contribute positively to your life and those who may evoke feelings of frustration or unhappiness. Use this to guide your decisions about which connections to maintain, nurture, or even release from your life.

4. Since relationships can evolve, it's important to continually reassess their influence on your emotions and life. Spend time reflecting every few months to ensure your relationships continue

to serve you well.

When you evaluate the emotional weight of your relationships, you become equipped with the knowledge needed to make intentional decisions. You gain clarity about who enriches your life, which helps you to create a more supportive social circle aligned with self-love.

Surround Yourself with Positivity

Positive influences in your life can enhance your self-love and emotional resilience. Surrounding yourself with supportive individuals boosts your ability to combat self-doubt and reinforces your self-worth. Positive relationships inspire and motivate personal growth, which empowers you to embrace new experiences and step outside your comfort zone.

A supportive network helps to overcome self-doubt and feelings of isolation. Other people can help you believe and love yourself by reminding you that you are not alone in your struggles. Give yourself permission to prioritize connections that improve your emotional well-being and bring joy into your life.

Spend a few moments reflecting on your current social circle and identifying individuals who uplift and inspire you. Those are connections that affirm your worth and encourage you to pursue your passions and interests. Interacting with people who celebrate your achievements provides you with the motivation to continue moving forward on your journey.

Positive relationships can take many forms, such as friends, mentors, colleagues, or community members who share your values and goals. Attend local groups, workshops, or events that resonate with your interests, and actively engage with others who support you. You can also join clubs or online communities where you can connect with like-minded individuals who share your aspirations and dreams.

As you surround yourself with positivity, your environment becomes nurturing for your mental and emotional health. It allows you to thrive as you reclaim your self-love and embrace the authentic you. Each positive relationship becomes a building block in your support system, which contributes to your growth and fulfillment as you heal and discover more about yourself.

Communicate Self-Worth with Confidence

Self-love requires that you communicate your self-worth to others confidently. When you express your value clearly and assertively, you affirm your self-worth and set the tone for how others perceive and interact with you. Confidence in communication means learning to articulate your needs, desires, and boundaries with clarity and assertiveness. It involves recognizing that your voice deserves to be heard and that your feelings are valid. This empowering practice creates an environment where you and those around you have relationships built on respect and mutual understanding.

The Power of Authentic Communication

Communicating with authenticity helps establish strong relationships and increases self-worth. Being genuine in your interactions leads to an atmosphere of trust and connection where both you and others feel more comfortable and valued. Authenticity strengthens the foundation of your relationships by encouraging honest discussions and reinforcing your confidence in expressing your feelings and needs.

Honest communication nurtures stronger emotional bonds and helps in building a supportive network where everyone feels safe to share their experiences. If others see you communicating freely, you also invite them to share their true selves, resulting in a more enriching and meaningful exchange. This authenticity encourages vulnerability, creating a safe space for sharing thoughts and emotions without fear of judgment.

You can practice authentic communication by focusing on your own feelings and experiences. Make a conscious effort to speak from the heart and express your thoughts and emotions clearly. Set clear intentions about what you want to communicate before you have deep conversations. Whether it's expressing a need or sharing a concern, knowing your intention can guide your words and help convey your self-worth effectively.

Expressing Feelings Openly

Learning to share your feelings openly helps with developing supportive relationships. The ability to express emotions can deepen connections and improve mutual understanding, which opens you up to more fulfilling interactions. Communicating openly can clarify your needs and eliminate assumptions that previously led to misunderstandings and conflict.

Effectively express your feelings by identifying what you're experiencing. Take time to reflect on your emotions before discussing them: Are you feeling happy, anxious, or overwhelmed? Once you have a clearer perspective, practice articulating your feelings using "I" statements. For example, instead of saying, "You never listen to me," you might express, "I feel unheard when my thoughts are overlooked." This approach helps communicate your needs without assigning blame and makes it easier for others to understand your perspective.

Be vulnerable as you share your thoughts and feelings honestly. The more you practice this skill, the more comfortable you will become in expressing your feelings and reinforcing your sense of self-worth. Remember, vulnerability can demonstrate strength rather than weakness. Sharing your feelings openly can build deeper connections in an environment of trust.

Active Listening

Active listening is a skill that enhances your relationships because you are present and fully engaged in conversations, which strengthens your connection with others. Active listening involves hearing the words people say and understanding the emotions and intentions behind them.

Active listening nurtures an environment where all feelings are validated and respected. It focuses on two-way dialogue that increases emotional safety and allows both of you to share openly without worrying about being dismissed.

To become an active listener:

- Create a safe space where both of you feel comfortable sharing your feelings.

- Focus on the speaker and avoid distractions.

- Maintain eye contact.

- Nod to show understanding.

- Minimize interruptions.

- Rephrase what the other person said to confirm your understanding. For instance, you might say, "What I'm hearing is that you feel overwhelmed by your current situation."

Practicing active listening demonstrates your commitment to the conversation and shows respect for the other person's feelings. Continuously check in with your friends about their comfort levels in discussing certain topics, and share how you are experiencing the conversation. This enables mutual understanding and respect.

Create a Feedback Loop

Healthy relationships thrive on constructive feedback, which is necessary for personal and mutual growth. Sharing constructive feedback can help you and the other person grow. It's about being honest with each other, acknowledging faults, and choosing to change for the better. Openly discussing observations or concerns can lead to positive changes that improve the quality of your interactions.

A feedback loop can help you to implement constructive input from others. You can ask others how you can improve, receive feedback, and make the necessary changes. And then the whole process starts again, resulting in a continuous loop where you listen to others, nurture self-acceptance, and learn to love yourself. In the same way, you will also give feedback and support others.

Keep the following in mind:

- Be specific and objective when giving feedback. Use "I" statements to express how certain behaviors affect you, such as, "I felt disappointed when our plans changed last minute." This approach invites conversation rather than defensiveness and allows the other person to understand your perspective without feeling attacked. Invite them to share their perspective on the situation for a constructive dialogue.

- Be open to receiving feedback and try to listen without becoming defensive. Acknowledge the feelings behind the feedback, and think about how it can strengthen your relationship. Showing openness to feedback demonstrates a commitment to mutual improvement.

- Check in with your friends or partners frequently to discuss your relationship openly, set expectations, and address any concerns. This creates a supportive environment where both of you are acknowledged and valued, which enriches the connection.

Key Takeaways

Healthy connections from positive relationships can have a positive impact on building self-love. Surrounding yourself with individuals who uplift, support, and celebrate you is beneficial; it nurtures your emotional well-being and helps with reclaiming your sense of identity. These relationships require intention, openness, and vulnerability. Prioritizing connections built on mutual respect and understanding creates an environment for growth and resilience. As you move forward, stay mindful of the energy you bring to your relationships and the energy you allow into your life. There is beauty in shared experiences, but don't hesitate to set boundaries that protect your mental space. The love you develop within healthy relationships will reflect and increase the love you have for yourself, guiding you on your path toward joy and fulfillment.

Chapter Seven

Develop a Self-Love Routine

For many of us, our past experiences may have led to feelings of inadequacy and self-doubt. You can overcome this by taking intentional, nurturing steps. A self-love routine can help you prioritize your emotional well-being and create a protective barrier against the negative thoughts that may arise from your history. This chapter will guide you through practical strategies and exercises to integrate self-love into your daily life, so that you can reclaim your identity for a greater sense of joy and fulfillment.

Create a Daily Self-Care and Self-Love Practice

A daily self-care and self-love practice starts the process of building a healthier relationship with yourself. Carve out dedicated time each day for activities that inspire you and bring you joy, even if it's as simple as enjoying a quiet cup of tea. These small, consistent practices reinforce your worth and helps change negative thought patterns. Self-love is not achieved overnight; it's developed through patience and persistence. As you prioritize these moments of self-care, you'll find that your capacity to love yourself grows, which results in healing and a renewed sense of joy in your life.

Morning Rituals

Start your day with an intention to set a positive tone for everything that follows throughout the day.

A morning routine can include as many of the following as you want:

- Spend five to ten minutes on meditation. Find a quiet space, close your eyes, and focus on your breath. If your mind wanders, gently bring your attention back to your breathing without judging yourself or your thoughts. Meditation increases self-awareness and helps you center your thoughts, which allows you to approach the day with clarity and calmness.

- After meditation, allocate a few minutes to writing down or capturing your thoughts.

- Create a simple list of intentions or goals for the day. Outline specific tasks to provide yourself with a plan for success. These intentions can be as straightforward as "take a ten-minute walk" or "reach out to a friend." Starting your day with clear intentions can improve your mood and productivity.

- Personalize your morning routine by adding activities that you love. This may include enjoying a smoothie, reading an inspiring book, or doing light stretching or yoga. Whatever resonates with you, make sure it is a part of your morning ritual, as consistency helps establish a dedicated self-love practice.

Mindful Breaks

Mindful breaks can help you achieve emotional balance and prevent burnout. These short pauses allow you to recalibrate and refresh your mind.

Some tips for mindful breaks:

- Set reminders on your phone or use timers to schedule short breaks throughout your day. Allocate 5–15 minutes for each break, depending on your schedule. Use this time to step away from work, and use it to breathe, and reconnect with yourself.

- Spend your breaks doing self-care activities that nourish you. For example, take a quick walk outside, stretch, or listen to your favorite music. These activities help improve your mood and create a sense of calm amidst a busy day.

- Practice deep breathing exercises during breaks. You can use the 4–7–8 method from Chapter 3. This technique can help reduce stress and anxiety to keep you centered and focused.

Evening Reflective Practices

Reflective practices can be used before bed to promote relaxation and self-acceptance. These rituals offer an opportunity to unwind and acknowledge your daily achievements.

Your evening routine can include several elements:

- Dedicate a few moments each night to reflect on your day. You can do this by writing down three things you accomplished or were grateful for throughout the day. It's okay to also mention any challenges and how you overcame them. Reflecting helps create a sense of fulfillment and gratitude, which encourages a more positive mindset.

- Design a calming routine that signals to your body that it's time to wind down. This might include activities like reading, taking a warm bath, or drinking calming tea. The objective is to create an environment conducive to relaxation that allows your mind to shift into rest mode.

- Self-acceptance exercises can be added to your evening routine. Just a few minutes spent focusing on your strengths and qualities that you admire brings about gratitude, reinforces positive self-perceptions, and builds love for who you are.

- Set a sleep schedule that gives you enough time for adequate rest. Prioritize your sleep environment by keeping your bedroom dark and quiet. You can do some calming activities before bed to prepare your mind for restful sleep.

Weekly Self-Care Assessments

It helps to allocate time to assessing your self-care routine as it supports continued growth and accountability. The more you adapt your routine to fit your life, the more resilient and flexible you become. This reflection helps you adapt to your changing needs and increases resilience.

Activities for a weekly self-care assessment:

- Choose a specific day each week to evaluate your self-care practices. Reflect on what worked well and what may need to be removed from your schedule or changed to better suit your needs. You can dedicate an area in your journal to log your feelings, activities, and progress.

- Use weekly assessments to hold yourself accountable for your self-love progress. Celebrate your successes–even tiny steps–and acknowledge areas that may need more attention or that you find challenging. This process helps you take ownership of your self-care practices.

- Self-care routines are not one-size-fits-all; they should change as you grow. If you notice certain activities are no longer serving you, be open to trying new activities that may better align with your current needs and preferences.

Affirmations, Journaling, and Mindfulness for Self-Reflection

Self-reflection and growth are possible with various strategies like affirmations, journaling, and mindfulness. These all contribute to a positive self-image and improved emotional well-being. When combined with your self-care routine, these practices create a holistic approach to nurture your mental health, build resilience, and lay a foundation for self-love. Together, they empower you to embrace your true self and face the challenges of life confidently.

Personalized Affirmations

The more personal and meaningful the affirmations, the more impactful they will be. Customizing your affirmations helps you affirm specific qualities and establish a strong emotional connection to yourself. This connection increases their effectiveness and reliability, making affirmations a valuable part of your daily routine.

Steps to personalize affirmations:

1. Reflect on aspects of your self-image you want to improve. Are there particular insecurities you wish to address? Or perhaps strengths you want to celebrate? What are some qualities you want to work on?

2. Write affirmations that align with the insights you've gained. For example, if you struggle with self-doubt, an affirmation may be, "I trust my abilities and decision-making."

3. Ensure your affirmations are framed in a positive light and stated in the present tense. This reinforces the belief that you are already embodying the qualities you wish to affirm.

4. Commit to reciting your affirmations consistently. Place them where you will see them often—like on your bathroom mirror, in your journal, or as reminders on your phone.

5. Let your affirmations evolve with you. As you grow, revisit and refresh them to stay aligned with your healing process.

Daily Journaling Practices

Choose a dedicated time each day for journaling; make it a non-negotiable part of your self-care. Consistent journaling increases your self-awareness and helps with personal growth over time. This allows you to celebrate achievements and encourages you to confront and learn from setbacks.

Here are some tips:

- Use a few minutes every morning to journal about your intentions for the day. Write down your goals and affirmations to set the stage for how you want to feel and act.

- Schedule times throughout your day for quick emotional check-ins. Write down what you're feeling and why, which helps to process and validate your emotions in real-time.

- Dedicate time each evening to reflect on the day's events. Journal about what went well and what challenges you faced while celebrating your efforts and learning from experiences.

- Use prompts like "What did I learn about myself today?" or "What am I grateful for?" or "Write down something positive about yourself each day," to explore areas you may not have considered.

- Reflect on how different experiences make you feel by using all your senses. Write about the sights, sounds, and emotions associated with your thoughts to deepen your reflections.

Mindful Reflection with Affirmations

Affirmations become more impactful when you pair them with mindfulness. The idea is to be fully present in the moment and acknowledge your thoughts and feelings without judgment. Repeating affirmations while being mindful can increase their emotional resonance and impact in your daily life.

To pair affirmations and mindfulness:

1. Before reciting your affirmations, take a few deep breaths. Ground yourself in the present moment and allow distractions to fade away.

2. Repeat your affirmations and focus on the meaning behind each word. Feel the emotions associated with them; embrace the positivity and empowerment they ignite in you.

3. Visualize yourself embodying the qualities you are speaking about in your affirmations. Imagine how you would feel and behave with confidence and self-love.

4. If you want to, you can include mindfulness meditation or yoga in your routine.

5. After affirming your qualities, take a moment to express gratitude for these attributes. Immerse yourself in a sense of appreciation for who you are and your journey.

Physical Health and Mental Well-Being

Taking care of your physical health is crucial for positive mental well-being. When you take care of your body, you also improve your mind. Regular exercise, balanced nutrition, and getting enough sleep have an effect on your mood, reduce stress, and improve mental clarity (Green, 2023). Making self-care a priority for both your physical and emotional health helps you recognize that self-love involves taking care of every part of yourself. This balanced approach helps you feel better overall, enabling you to lead a happier and more fulfilling life.

Nutrition

Nutrition affects your overall mood and energy levels. What you eat can significantly impact how you feel. Nourishing your body with wholesome, nutrient-rich foods supports mental clarity and emotional stability (Muscaritoli, 2021). Aim to incorporate a variety of fruits, vegetables, whole grains, and healthy fats into your daily meals, as these foods provide essential vitamins and minerals that contribute to mood regulation.

Keep the following in mind:

- Pay attention to how different foods make you feel. Are there certain meals that boost your energy or lift your spirits?

- Plan your meals ahead of time, as it makes it easier to choose healthy options when hunger strikes. You may want to prepare snacks, like sliced vegetables or fruit, to have on hand and support your balanced lifestyle.

- Cooking can be a form of self-care and bring you joy. Experiment with new recipes or prepare your favorites to turn meal preparation into an enjoyable activity. The cooking process can help you establish a positive relationship with food and encourage mindfulness as you nourish your body.

- Don't forget to hydrate. Drinking enough water throughout the day can impact your energy levels and mood. Keep a water bottle with you as a reminder to stay hydrated, and set goals for your water intake to help stick to this habit.

Exercise

Physical activity can be a form of self-care. Exercise helps you stay fit and celebrates your body's role in emotional wellness. Physical activity stimulates the release of endorphins, often referred to as "feel-good" hormones, which elevate your mood and reduce feelings of anxiety (Raypole, 2022).

Best practices for combining self-care and exercise:

- Aim for at least 30 minutes of moderate exercise most days of the week. It can be swimming, dancing, walking, or participating in a sports activity you enjoy.

- Stop thinking about physical activity as punishment and consider it a celebration. Workouts aren't chores; they are a way to honor your body. Celebrate what your body can do to foster body positivity.

- Find activities that bring you enjoyment. Whether it's yoga, weight lifting, Pilates, pickleball, or hiking, choosing fun exercises can make physical health enjoyable and sustainable. You can also join classes or community groups to provide social support and motivation that helps you stay committed to your routine.

- Listen to your body and pay attention to how it feels during and after exercise. If you're tired, take a rest day or do a low-intensity workout. Up the energy on days when you are feeling good. Your routine should respect your body's signals and positively influence your wellness journey.

Sleep Hygiene

A good night's rest impacts your physical and mental health. Quality sleep improves your cognitive function, emotional regulation, and overall well-being (Ramar, et al., 2021). When you prioritize adequate rest, you're actively caring for yourself and reinforcing the idea that you deserve to feel your best.

Your sleep matters:

- Aim for 7–9 hours of sleep each night by going to bed and waking up at the same time every day. A consistent sleep schedule helps regulate your body's internal clock and improves the quality of your sleep.

- Create a calming bedtime routine that signals to your body that it's time to wind down. This may include activities like reading, practicing relaxation techniques, or taking a warm bath. Try to limit screen time at least an hour before bed to reduce blue light exposure, as this can interfere with your ability to fall asleep.

- Ensure your sleep environment is comfortable and conducive to rest. Keep your bedroom dark, quiet, and cool. You may want to use earplugs, an eye mask, or a white noise machine to create a peaceful atmosphere.

Mind-Body Practices

Mind-body practices can enhance your physical and mental well-being. They help you to relax, reduce stress, and strengthen the connection between body and mind (McGarvie, 2025).

Some methods to incorporate mind and body:

- Explore yoga or tai chi, as both combine physical movement, breath control, and mindfulness. These practices increase relaxation and balance, which helps you connect with your body and reduce stress.

- Engage in mindfulness exercises throughout the day. Simple techniques like focusing on your breath, mindful walking, or savoring a meal can help ground you in the present moment and enhance the connection between body and mind.

- Develop a regular mind-body routine that includes practices you enjoy. You may want to try a weekly yoga class, daily stretching, or meditation sessions. Keep exploring to find activities that resonate with you and strengthen your self-love.

- Attend workshops, classes, or online sessions that introduce you to new techniques.

Key Takeaways

Developing self-love through intentional self-care practices is part of the process to build emotional resilience and experience personal growth. Prioritizing your well-being and nurturing your relationship with yourself creates a strong basis for a happier and more fulfilling life. Have patience, compassion, and dedication for yourself. Celebrate the small victories along the way, and be gentle with yourself during tough moments. The more you work on self-love, the more you empower yourself to embrace your true identity, unlock your potential, and cultivate joy in every aspect of your life. You are deserving of love, respect, and happiness, so continue to invest in yourself and nurture the incredible person you are.

Chapter Eight

Overcoming Obstacles to Self-Love

Obstacles can stand in our way and cast shadows on our true potential as we search for self-love. These challenges can stem from deep-rooted beliefs, past wounds, and the societal pressures that influence our perception of self-worth. As you work through this chapter, you'll discover the common barriers that prevent progress, like self-doubt, perfectionism, and the lingering effects of toxic relationships. But you can overcome adversity by embracing your past as a part of your story. You have the strength to rise above these challenges, and with each small victory, you'll move closer to accepting and loving yourself.

How to Handle Setbacks and Moments of Self-Doubt

Setbacks and moments of self-doubt are inevitable as you learn to love yourself, but they don't define your worth or journey. These feelings are important, as they often signal areas that need healing and attention. Instead of letting doubt consume you, you can work through it with compassion and resilience. Your setbacks are opportunities for growth rather than failures. There are strategies to confront and manage these feelings, which empower you to move forward with confidence.

Common Triggers

Everyone faces specific scenarios that can ignite feelings of inadequacy. These may include receiving critical feedback at work, encountering a social setting that stirs anxiety, or comparing yourself to peers or friends who seem more accomplished. Identifying these triggers can prepare you to deal with them more effectively. Self-doubt is a natural human experience, and acknowledging this can help normalize these feelings; it doesn't make you weak or unworthy. These feelings come from your innate desire for acceptance and love.

You can develop a personal plan that outlines how you will confront triggers:

- Write down the situations where self-doubt creeps in. Are you at home, with specific people, or surrounded by a challenging environment? Reflect on how you felt and reacted. For example, if you know that social gatherings often lead to feelings of inadequacy, prepare for these events by practicing positive affirmations in advance.

- Remind yourself of your worth and capabilities before stepping into triggering situations. This might involve preparing affirmations to tell yourself before entering a triggering situation or envisioning a positive outcome.

- When self-doubt arises, remind yourself that everyone faces setbacks. Acknowledge your feelings without judgment and understand that these moments are temporary and do not define your value.

- Think about setbacks as learning opportunities. Setbacks can increase personal growth and lead to better resilience. Reflect on them and identify the valuable lessons that help you progress with self-love.

Developing a Self-Check Routine

A regular self-assessment routine can increase your self-awareness during challenging times. A self-check routine can give you insights into your life and enable you to move on.

Make an Appointment With Yourself

Schedule time weekly to reflect on your thoughts, feelings, and emotional state. This dedicated time for introspection allows you to catch negative patterns early and make the necessary changes before things spiral out of control. You can use a planner or journal where you document your feelings and experiences.

Positive Affirmations

Create a checklist of positive affirmations that speak to your needs and growth. For instance, whenever self-doubt starts creeping in, remind yourself about your abilities by repeating phrases like, "I can do this," "I deserve positive outcomes," and "I have overcome challenges before." Keep this checklist handy and recite these affirmations frequently to internalize their positivity.

Turn to Prior Successes

Make it a habit to write down moments when you triumphed, even if it's just small things. For instance, completing a difficult project at work or nurturing a relationship. Whenever self-doubt creeps in, revisit these memories to remind yourself of what you are capable of achieving.

Commit and Permit

Set a timeframe for your self-assessment to help reduce the impact of long periods of self-doubt. Make it a commitment to regularly check in with yourself and analyze your feelings. It's okay to feel doubt, but don't allow it to linger any longer than necessary. The idea is to create an environment that nurtures your emotional health and develops a positive relationship with yourself.

Mindfulness Techniques

Mindfulness techniques can make a difference during moments of insecurity. They ground you in the present moment and reduce anxiety associated with self-doubt.

Some mindfulness practices you may want to include in your day:

- Simple deep breathing exercises can calm your mind, give you clarity, and allow self-compassion to surface.

- A few minutes of meditation, focused breathing, and stillness can help you gain perspective when you're feeling overwhelmed. Consistent meditation increases self-awareness and enables you to observe your thoughts without judgment.

- Mindfulness apps offer guided meditations and exercises that have been designed to combat self-doubt and increase self-love. These resources provide structure to your practice, make it easier to be mindful daily, and you can use them wherever you go.

- Write, dance, draw, or use any other form of creativity to understand what you're going through, allowing yourself to release negative feelings and observe patterns in your emotional responses.

Relying on Others

A support system can reduce feelings of isolation during challenging times. People who understand you can provide solace during moments of self-doubt. Be vulnerable with your support network, and they will help you heal, as sharing your struggles can strengthen connections and compassionate support. Reaching out for help can be as basic as a text or phone call. Share your thoughts and feelings with them, as verbalizing your challenges can lessen their weight and turn feelings of isolation into feelings of connection and understanding. Your friends can offer different perspectives and help you see that many others face similar issues and emotions.

If you want to, you can join support groups, either in-person or online, where people come together to share their experiences and motivate one another. Being part of a community that focuses on self-improvement and emotional health can reinforce your progress towards self-love.

Don't shy away from seeking professional help if you find yourself feeling overwhelmed by self-doubt or struggling to cope with it. A therapist or counselor can share valuable tools and strategies based on your unique experiences. They can guide you in learning more effective coping mechanisms and provide different viewpoints on the challenges you face. Know that asking for help is not a sign of weakness; rather, it's a way to achieve self-acceptance and proof of your commitment to growth.

Managing Societal Pressures and External Criticism

We are constantly bombarded with messages about how we should look, act, and feel, often leading to unrealistic comparisons that can be damaging to our sense of self-worth. The voices of others can reverberate deeply and cause feelings of inadequacy and self-doubt. These norms are constructed from narrow perspectives that rarely capture the complexity of human experiences. They lead to criticisms that may come from insecurities and experiences, not your worth.

But are these messages and expectations true? It's important to question their validity. Ask yourself: "Do these expectations align with who I am?" As you realize that many societal standards are unattainable and often contradictory, you permit yourself to grow your way. This self-acceptance encourages authenticity, allowing you to define your worth by your standards. Your value is not determined by how closely you conform to external criteria; they are defined by the unique qualities that make you, you.

Critical Thinking

Critical thinking skills can help you manage external messages. The ability to assess feedback develops personal resilience and empowers you to take control of your story.

Here are some strategies to improve your critical thinking:

- Evaluate the motives behind the criticism you receive. Is the feedback coming from a place of care, or is it perhaps motivated by the critic's insecurities?

- Distinguish between constructive and destructive feedback to change how you respond. Constructive feedback is intended to help you grow, while destructive criticism tends to diminish your confidence. Ask yourself whether the criticism offers actionable insights or aims to undermine your self-esteem.

- Adopt a growth mindset instead of viewing feedback as personal attacks. Reframe how you interpret criticism by asking questions such as: "What can I learn from this?" or "How can this feedback help me become a better version of myself?"

- Use a "feedback journal" or any other place you can capture your thoughts can help. Make a note of the criticism you receive along with your reflections to get clarity on what feedback is useful and what should be dismissed.

Personal Boundaries

Clear boundaries should be set with people who impose societal expectations. This protects your self-esteem. Learning how to say "no" without guilt is an empowering practice. You have the right to set limits on what you allow in terms of feedback to create a more nurturing environment for yourself. You don't have to be closed off to constructive criticism, but you can protect yourself from negativity that doesn't serve your well-being.

In Chapter 6, we discussed setting boundaries, so have a look back at those strategies and tips. When it comes to expectations, feedback, and boundaries, identify the types of interactions that drain your energy or make you feel less than worthy. Are there friends or acquaintances who consistently impose unrealistic standards on you? If so, think about how you can create distance or set firm boundaries with them. This may mean politely declining invitations to discussions that lead to comparisons, or limiting the time you spend with people who contribute to your insecurities.

Express your boundaries confidently in these circumstances. Practice using phrases like, "I appreciate your concern, but I am focusing on my growth," or "I need to prioritize my mental health right now." This practice protects your self-esteem and nurtures healthier relationships that respect who you are and what you value.

Champion Your Story

Your narrative can be a powerful antidote to external pressures. You have a unique story that adds richness to your identity. Sharing your experiences, both the struggles and triumphs, can create connections with others and lead to a community centered around understanding and support.

Celebrate yourself and the small victories that mark your growth. Your accomplishment list or any other journal is a great place to record your challenges and achievements. This can be motivating, as it enables you to see how far you've come over time. Reflect on these moments to remind yourself that your journey is characterized by progress, even when it feels slow.

Your personal growth story has the potential to inspire others, too. When you share your narrative, you become a symbol of hope for those experiencing similar circumstances. Conversations about your life can reaffirm your self-worth while motivating others to embrace their stories. It also provides solace and develops a sense of camaraderie when you connect and share with others.

Community activities or platforms focused on sharing personal stories can deepen these connections. You could join a storytelling group or participate in panels that emphasize the importance of individual experiences. These opportunities enrich your self-esteem and remind you that vulnerability can boost strength and resilience.

As you engage with your narrative, take notice of how it feels. Are there still lingering societal expectations tugging at your emotions? Address these feelings head-on to reclaim your story fully, ensuring that it is yours and yours alone. The more you honor your story, the more empowered you'll feel to accept your identity without external influence.

Staying Committed to Personal Growth

Personal growth requires consistent commitment. The concept of continual self-improvement allows you to evolve and adapt, which gives you a better understanding of who you are and what you want from life. This commitment empowers you to break free from limiting beliefs and reinforces your self-worth and resilience. As you go through the process of self-discovery, you develop a mindset that celebrates progress, including the little things.

Work Toward Your Goals

Achievable, incremental goals can help you sustain your personal growth. It starts with breaking larger aspirations into smaller, manageable milestones. For instance, if your goal is to improve your communication, you can set a target of meeting with one person weekly instead of committing to large social gatherings. These smaller goals are more attainable and help build momentum as you experience small wins. As you achieve smaller objectives, celebrate these milestones to reinforce your motivation. Instead of chasing perfection, redirect your focus toward the process of growth. Improvement takes time, and it's natural to make mistakes along the way. Have self-compassion as you improve yourself to ensure you stay motivated while remembering that each small step contributes to your progress.

Reflect Frequently

Occasional self-assessment can support your long-term commitment to personal growth. Use this time to consider what you have learned about yourself, your strengths, and the areas where you can continue to grow.

These reflection sessions enable you to recalibrate your goals as needed. Capture your thoughts, feelings, and experiences related to your growth. Think about things like what you learned this week, the challenges you faced, and how you overcame them. Review your past entries to better understand how you are changing.

Find Accountability Partners

Involving others in your growth can enhance your commitment and motivation. Look for accountability partners who share similar goals or interests or who have also experienced similar circumstances. This partnership produces a supportive environment that motivates you to stay on track and continue growing together.

Make the most of your accountability partnership:

- Set mutual goals with your accountability partner.

- Establish a consistent check-in schedule, whether it's weekly or monthly appointments.

- Share progress, discuss challenges, and celebrate victories to provide motivation and a sense of belonging.

- Create a comfortable space for vulnerability and meaningful conversations with your partner.

- Be open about your struggles and achievements, and encourage your partner to do the same.

Key Takeaways

Facing obstacles to self-love requires patience, intention, and a commitment to personal growth. As you deal with self-doubt, societal pressures, and past wounds, remember that each step you take helps you heal, stimulates growth, and becomes part of your story. As you develop compassion for yourself, you prioritize your emotional well-being and unlock the incredible strength that self-love brings. Your journey is uniquely yours, and every effort you make to nurture self-love adds to your resilience and worthiness. Keep an open heart and maintain the unwavering belief that you deserve love, starting with yourself.

Chapter Nine

Living Authentically

Living authentically means accepting and loving who you are and aligning your life with your core values. You shed the masks you've worn to please others and allow them to see your genuine self. It can be scary, especially when faced with expectations and judgments. However, authenticity opens the door to self-acceptance, joy, and fulfillment. In this chapter, you'll explore what it means to live in alignment with your true values. You'll reflect on the importance of self-awareness, understand how to identify your values, and learn strategies to make them part of your daily life. You can reclaim your identity, improve your emotional well-being, and create a life that reflects your passions and desires.

Let Your Actions Speak Your Values

Your core beliefs and values are guides for authenticity and personal fulfillment. Every day, your actions should reflect your true self, so that you have a sense of integrity and purpose. This alignment can improve your self-esteem and build trust in your relationships, as others can sense your genuineness. Your values empower you to make decisions that support your well-being and happiness, which allows you to have a more meaningful life where you act with confidence and clarity.

What Are Your Core Values?

Authenticity and alignment begin with an understanding of your personal values. It helps to create a list of values that reverberate with you, such as honesty, creativity, compassion, or freedom. Narrow this list down to your top five core values, the ones that feel non-negotiable in your life, and reflect on why these values matter to you and how they influence your decisions and interactions.

The following strategies can help you identify your core values:

- What values were evident during these moments?

- How did these experiences affect your beliefs and priorities?

- Did you feel fulfilled or proud in any particular situation? Why?

- Reflect on anything that inspires or motivates you, like people, books, movies, or quotes. Determine what you admire about these people or things and the qualities they embody. Then, think about why these attributes appeal to you.

- Use a values assessment tool, which can guide you in identifying your core values. There are also various resources available online that will provide you with a comprehensive list of common values. Review each value and consider whether it describes you and the life you want to live.

- Imagine your ideal life five or ten years from now. Envision what it looks like, how it feels, and what values are reflected in that vision. Write a description of what you see and emphasize the aspects that reflect your core self.

- Reflect on experiences or areas in your life where you feel dissatisfaction or frustration. Consider:

  -

  - What is triggering this discontent?

  - Which of your values are not being honored in these situations?

  - What changes can you make to realign your actions with your values?

  -

  - What makes me feel fulfilled?

  - What do I want to prioritize in my life?

  - How do I want to be remembered by others?

  - Ask trusted friends or family members what they perceive as your strengths and core principles. You can also ask them what words they think of when they hear your name. Their perspective may pinpoint values you've overlooked or taken for granted.

You can use any of these strategies to identify your values. Once you do, experiment with your values in real-world situations. Participate in activities that align with your ideas and observe how they make you feel. This experiential approach can help you affirm your values and recognize what feels most like you.

But what about your current behaviors? Do your daily actions reflect your core values? Identify areas where there may be misalignment and consider what changes you can make to bring your actions in line with your beliefs. This alignment positively affects your self-esteem and emotional resilience, which enables you to face life's inevitable ups and downs.

Embody Your Values

A personalized action plan helps translate your values into daily behaviors that give you purpose and direction. It allows you to live out what matters to you, so that you have a better sense of self.

Create your action plan:

1. Define clear goals that reflect your core values. Instead of vague objectives, use the SMART criteria (Specific, Measurable, Achievable, Relevant, Time-bound) to give you concrete guidance. For example, if "community" is a core value, instead of saying "I want to help others," you can say, "I will volunteer at the local food bank for two hours every Saturday for the next three months."

2. Deconstruct your goals and turn them into actionable steps that feel manageable and relevant. For example, for a stress-reduction goal, your action steps might include meditating each day, prioritizing self-care, and scheduling a weekly therapy session to work through your emotions.

3. Decide on a realistic timeline for each action step. However, make these deadlines emotionally significant by associating them with your aspirations. For instance, if your value of "personal growth"

involves reading, set a goal to complete one personal development book every month.

4. Create a value-based routine based on your goals and what you want to achieve. Designate specific times for actions and activities that reflect your values. For example, if "creativity" is important to you, schedule an hour on Saturday mornings to explore painting, writing, or hobbies you're passionate about.

5. Use visual aids like a vision board or a tracking journal. This becomes a constant reminder of what you are working toward and helps you stay motivated. Record your journey by capturing milestones, setbacks, and personal revelations along the way.

6. Share your action plan with someone who understands your life and will be there for you. Discuss your goals and progress, including challenges, so that you can support each other as you align your life with your values.

7. Set aside time each month to revisit your action plan and reflect on your experiences. Assess what worked, what didn't, and how you felt about the actions you took. How did your activities and decisions embody your values?

8. Life is fluid, and sometimes your values may change based on new experiences or insights. Your action plan is a living document that you can adjust as needed. If a certain value or action no longer fits your lifestyle, don't hesitate to revise it.

9. Celebrate every little bit of progress. Create personal rituals for acknowledging your efforts, such as treating yourself to a special

outing, sharing your success with others, or enjoying a quiet moment of gratitude.

Your personalized action plan can effectively translate your core values into daily behaviors that honor who you are. This actionable approach leads to a sense of purpose and empowers you to build a life filled with self-love and authenticity.

Stay Aligned

Getting your values and actions to match up is an ongoing process that requires frequent reflection and self-assessment. Spend some time each week or month to evaluate whether your actions are in sync with your core beliefs.

Ask yourself the following questions:

- Are my current choices reflecting my values?

- Have I noticed any misalignments? Did I do anything that doesn't fit with my values?

- What can I adjust to remain true to myself?

Reflection creates opportunities to correct your efforts and grow because you know that setbacks happen but can be overcome. This kind of flexibility helps you adapt to changing circumstances and ensures you stay grounded in yourself.

The Benefits of Living Authentically

Living according to your values has numerous benefits. Authenticity enables higher self-esteem and confidence. You boost your sense of self-worth when you live in alignment with who you really are. Authentic living also leads to stronger connections with yourself and others. Being true to yourself attracts relationships that are based on honesty and mutual respect. You invite others to connect with you on a genuine level, which cultivates bonds that enrich your life.

Committing to authenticity equips you with resilience in the face of adversity. When challenges arise—and they will—your values can guide you to tackle difficulties with greater ease. Instead of being swayed by external pressures, you can draw upon your core beliefs to make decisions that support your well-being. The path to self-love and emotional independence begins with the commitment to live authentically—after all, you deserve to thrive and be unapologetically you!

Vulnerability Is a Strength

Vulnerability is often mistaken for weakness, but it is a courageous step toward authenticity. It requires the willingness to expose your true self, with all its imperfections and insecurities, resulting in genuine emotional expression.

Vulnerability is necessary if you want to be yourself fully. You have to allow yourself to be open about your fears, insecurities, and struggles, which creates a space for honest dialogue and deeper understanding. Vulnerability breaks down barriers, and acknowledging your imperfections demonstrates that it's okay to be human, inspiring those around you to do the same. This shared openness leads to trust and empathy.

By sharing your fears, struggles, and desires, you portray emotional honesty, which improves the quality of your relationships. Authenticity nurtures a sense of belonging and acceptance, and reminds you that everyone experiences insecurities. This makes it easier to connect on a more profound level. Vulnerability can change both how you see yourself and how others relate to you.

Vulnerability Has Value

Vulnerability comes with many psychological and emotional advantages (Moore, 2022). Firstly, taking emotional risks results in personal growth and resilience. You develop a strength that emphasizes self-awareness and adaptability when you allow yourself to be open and honest.

Sharing your vulnerabilities with other people also leads to empathy and understanding in relationships. Expressing your feelings creates an opportunity for others to be open with you, which strengthens emotional bonds and trust. This mutual sharing generates a sense of safety and support in your relationships.

Self-compassion and less self-judgment occur when you accept vulnerability. You don't have to think of your flaws as liabilities; instead, you see them as part of being human. This perspective nurtures a kinder relationship with yourself, helping with improved emotional well-being and inner peace.

How To Be More Vulnerable

Vulnerability requires an environment where you feel safe to express yourself.

The following exercises can help you be more vulnerable:

- Share aspects of your personal story that highlight your vulnerabilities. You can talk about moments of failure, insecurity, or growth—anything that feels authentic to you. Sharing these stories—although difficult—enhances community and support, so that others can relate to and empathize with your experiences.

- Spend time reflecting on your vulnerabilities.

-

- What fears have held you back from being vulnerable?

- In what situations have you felt safest to express your true self?

- How can you have more courage to share about your life?

- Set small challenges for yourself to practice vulnerability in gradual steps. This could be expressing an opinion in a group setting, sharing a personal story during a gathering, or discussing your feelings about a sensitive topic with a close friend. Gradually increasing your comfort zone can help you develop the habit of being more vulnerable while feeling safe.

- Join a support group or community where emotional honesty and vulnerability are encouraged. Sharing your experiences in a safe space with others who understand your life can increase your self-acceptance and help you express your feelings more freely.

Reframe Cultural Narratives

Challenging societal misconceptions about vulnerability is important. Many cultures stigmatize being vulnerable and see emotional expression as a weakness. But reframing vulnerability as a strength can boost personal growth. It is possible to resist the pressure to conform to Stoic ideals and allow yourself to feel and express your emotions genuinely.

Vulnerability empowers you to redefine your narrative despite what those around you are saying. It's okay not to have it all figured out. Stepping away from preconceived ideas of strength gives you the freedom to explore yourself and live boldly, regardless of societal expectations. Reflect on the impact that external influences have had on your concept of vulnerability. Are there aspects you can change? Be brave and allow vulnerability to have a place in your life.

Own Your Story

Your story holds power, and owning it can bolster your self-acceptance and empowerment. Your life story, with its unique experiences, triumphs, and challenges, is integral to who you are. Taking ownership of your narrative allows you to reclaim your voice and authenticity; you get to define your identity on your terms. Your journey—with all its ups and downs—enables you to process your past, learn from it, and use it as a source of strength. This act of self-ownership builds resilience and opens the door to a more fulfilling life, rooted in your truth.

The Power of Storytelling

Your personal story plays a role in shaping your self-perception and identity. Every experience you have, whether joyous or challenging, contributes to the story of who you are. Your personal narrative helps with developing deeper self-awareness that allows you to see how your past experiences influence your thoughts, behaviors, and emotions today.

Acknowledging your story empowers you to frame your experiences positively. Instead of viewing hardships solely as obstacles, you can see them as opportunities for growth and resilience. This reframing helps you reclaim your personal power and enables you to take charge of your life and the way you view yourself. For instance, if you've faced adversity, you can use lessons from those experiences to change your current situation. This recognition turns struggles into valuable insights that contribute to your growth, leading to a sense of strength and agency.

Think about your story:

1. Identify key moments in your life that have influenced who you are. These experiences can include achievements, challenges, relationships, or moments of clarity. Write them down and consider how each has influenced your identity and beliefs.

2. As you reflect on these experiences, pay attention to the emotions they evoke. What feelings arise when you think about them? Your emotions allow you to connect more deeply with your story and help you articulate your experiences more authentically.

3. Although not every experience will be positive, try to find something valuable in each situation. What strengths did you display?

What lessons did you learn? Reframing enhances your resilience and empowers you to approach future challenges with a constructive mindset.

Rewriting Your Story

You can rewrite your story! This is important for your present and future, especially as you move on from your past. Rewriting your narrative is a transformative practice that enables you to redefine your identity, gives you a sense of agency and strength, and lets you be who you want to be.

Here's how to reshape your story:

1. Start by challenging any victim mentality you might have adopted. It's easy to feel powerless when reflecting on certain experiences, but remind yourself that you have the power to shape your own life. Do not focus on what's been done to you; instead, emphasize your role in overcoming challenges.

2. Look for significant turning points in your life—the moments when you made crucial decisions or experienced changes in perspective. What happened? How did these events affect you? These moments reinforce your growth and transformation, turning you into a more empowered version of yourself.

3. Use creative outlets like journaling, art, or storytelling to explore and redefine your story. Write about your experiences, uncover your feelings, and create illustrative representations of your life and its big moments. This creative process can help you visualize your evolution and solidify the new narrative you wish to adopt.

4. Write a revised version of your narrative that reflects your newfound agency and strength. Include the challenges you've faced, the lessons you've learned, and your vision for the future. Focus on what will happen rather than dwelling on the past. Think about your story as a living document that you can continue to edit and update as you grow.

5. With your new story in place, set intentions that align with it. What do you want to accomplish moving forward? What values do you want to embody? Use these clear intentions as a roadmap for the life you wish to create.

Share Your Story

You already know that vulnerability forms part of your personal narratives, specifically when it comes to sharing your story with others. It's a reminder that you are not alone on your journey. Choose environments where you feel safe and comfortable sharing your experiences, such as with a trusted friend, support group, or on a community platform.

Speak from the heart and share your truth without holding back. Authenticity resonates with others and allows them to connect with your experiences on a deeper level. Your vulnerabilities can inspire and encourage those who hear your story. Sharing your experiences increases self-acceptance, including for those around you. Your story can inspire others to reflect on their journeys, validating their feelings and supporting acceptance within the community. This ripple effect of sharing life stories creates a community grounded in honesty and vulnerability.

Reflection and Growth

Ongoing reflection on your story can help you grow continuously. As you continue to love yourself, it helps to stay aware of your progress through personal development and self-acceptance. Choose a reflection schedule that feels right for you. Use these moments to review your personal story, assess your growth, and identify areas you wish to develop further. This is also the time to recognize milestones, reinforcing your sense of accomplishment. You can use this as a reminder of how far you've come and find motivation in how your story is continuing to evolve.

Change is a natural part of life, so welcome the opportunity to rewrite your story in light of your growth. Connect your story with your values and principles to increase your sense of identity. Affirmations that align with your empowered story can be helpful; remember to repeat them regularly. You can create a narrative that celebrates your life and honors your authentic self.

Key Takeaways

Living authentically requires syncing up your life with your values. It's a continuous process. You consistently need to check in with yourself, nurture your inner voice, and make choices that align with who you intend to be. Each step you take toward authenticity brings you closer to a more fulfilled existence.

Challenges may appear as you shed old patterns and face external pressures, but these moments of discomfort are often signs of growth. By prioritizing your values, you create a deeper connection with yourself and those around you. Celebrate the unique qualities that make you who you are and be proud of the life you are creating. Let your true self guide you daily to experience a life filled with joy, purpose, and unshakeable self-love.

Chapter Ten

Sustaining Unapologetic Self-Love

Unapologetic self-love shifts your focus from the initial spark of self-acceptance to the long-term commitment of nurturing that love daily. Fleeting moments of empowerment are not enough; real change lies in maintaining and deepening this love, regardless of your past. This final chapter discusses the principles and practices required for continuous growth and resilience, allowing you to rise above prior wounds and negative self-perceptions. The commitment to yourself is a gift that keeps on giving.

Long-Term Self-Love Strategies

Unapologetic self-love requires a deliberate commitment to putting empowering practices into your daily life. These strategies reinforce the love you have for yourself and initiate growth and healing. Consistency is important because when you commit to these actions, they become a natural part of your routine. The key to sustained self-love is to remain proactive in your approach and to construct a supportive environment for growth, healing, and joy.

A Self-Love Manifesto

A personal self-love manifesto can establish a strong commitment to yourself. This manifesto is a declaration of your intrinsic worth and set of principles that guide your self-care practices.

Set aside some time to create a self-love manifesto:

1. Think deeply about what self-love means to you. What do you most value about yourself? What are your aspirations? Jot down key phrases or words that resonate strongly with you.

2. Write a series of affirmations and declarations that encapsulate your self-worth based on the phrases identified previously. These might include phrases like "I am worthy of love," "I embrace my imperfections," or "I can learn and grow from my experiences."

3. Design your manifesto creatively. Use colors, drawings, or images that inspire you, similar to what you would do with a vision board.

4. Place your manifesto where you can see it regularly, such as your mirror, desk, or fridge. Your manifesto is a daily reminder of your commitment to self-love.

5. Commit to reading your manifesto aloud to yourself daily. Internalize the words and recite them frequently to reinforce your self-worth.

6. As you grow and change, revisit your manifesto periodically. Reflect on how your self-love journey has changed, and adjust your

statements as necessary. This helps to keep your commitment fresh and relevant.

Your self-love manifesto is a guide for your thoughts and behaviors as you navigate the highs and lows of life.

Assess Your Progress

Self-reflection is part of growth. You need to monitor your progress actively, so that you can be motivated by it or correct course if necessary.

Self-reflection can be included in your routine:

1. Prepare a list of questions to help guide your reflections. For example:

2.

3. How do I feel about myself today?

4. What actions have I taken to nurture my self-love?

5. Have I encountered any negative thoughts? How did I respond to them?

6. What progress have I made?

7. What am I proud of?

8. Document your thoughts during these sessions in some way. Track any patterns you notice in your feelings or behaviors to reveal insights into areas where you may need to focus more attention.

9. Make it a point to acknowledge and celebrate your successes, no matter how small. Did you say no to something that drained your energy? Perhaps you took time for self-care when you needed it most. Write these victories down and appreciate the progress you've made.

10. Based on your reflections, identify if any practices need to be adjusted or replaced. If you find one approach isn't working for you anymore, be open to experimenting with new techniques. Being flexible keeps your self-love journey dynamic and effective.

11. Share your progress with a trusted friend or therapist to keep you accountable and get an external perspective.

Build a Self-Love Toolbox

A self-love toolbox is a collection of resources and techniques that you can draw upon whenever you need support. It keeps you going during difficult times.

Build your own self-love toolbox:

1. Make a list of people who can support you. They could be friends, family members, colleagues, or anyone else. Your support network should be able to help you with the needs you identified in the previous step.

2. Create a physical or digital binder containing resources associated with self-love. This could include:

3.

4. Your list of needs.

5. Ways to spend your time.

6. A list of people in your support network.

7. A curated playlist of uplifting songs.

8. Guided meditations or mindfulness exercises from apps or websites.

9. Inspirational quotes or images.

10. Worksheets or prompts for journaling or creativity.

11. Aim to include a variety of tools so that you have options depending on your mood. For instance, if you're feeling anxious, you might reach for a calming meditation. If you're experiencing a creative block, perhaps a coloring book or art supplies could help. And if you're feeling lonely, you may want to contact a friend.

12. Whenever you anticipate a stressful period—such as a busy work week—select specific strategies from your toolbox in advance. Being prepared allows you to practice self-care without hesitation and get support when you need it most.

13. Be open to new practices or tools to add to your toolbox. Attend new classes, read books, or participate in communities that focus on personal growth. You can diversify your skills and experience unexpected breakthroughs in your emotional health when you keep your toolbox relevant during changing circumstances.

A well-stocked self-love toolbox can help you manage daily life and keep you committed to ongoing self-love.

Lifelong Learning

Lifelong learning can reveal new ways to love yourself while focusing on personal growth. It can expand your understanding of what self-love means and how to practice it effectively.

Here are some places you can turn to for further education:

- Read books and articles on self-love, psychology, and emotional well-being. Create a reading list with a mix of theoretical knowledge and practical strategies to deepen your understanding of self-love concepts. You can also ask your therapist, support group, or other people which books they found enlightening.

- Attend local or online workshops focused on personal development. You will learn new concepts and strategies and connect with others who share similar experiences and goals.

- Podcasts and webinars often provide insights from experts who can offer valuable tips, new perspectives, and the latest research related to self-love and emotional health. They can introduce you to new strategies that may work for your needs.

- A support group or community focused on self-improvement can create connections that motivate you. Sharing experiences and learning from others is encouraging and holds you accountable.

- Reflect on what you learn and how you can apply new knowledge to your daily life. Update your self-love manifesto and toolkit based on these insights to solidify your commitment to lifelong learning.

- Be open to adapting your self-care practices as you acquire new knowledge. If you discover a new technique that appeals to you, add it to your routine. Lifelong learning gives you the flexibility needed to adjust your self-love strategy as your needs change.

Overcoming Personal Growth Plateaus

At various points in your life, you may feel like you are not progressing, like you are stuck. This is a plateau. They can feel frustrating and disheartening, but they are a natural part of self-love. These periods of stagnation may appear because you feel stuck or disconnected from the progress you've made. These plateaus are not failures, but they do give you time to reflect and adjust. You can identify the signs of stagnation, spot the underlying causes, and implement actionable steps to regain momentum.

Signs of a Plateau

To overcome a personal growth plateau, you have to recognize the signs that you're experiencing one. Knowing what stagnation looks like can empower you to take action.

Some common indicators to watch for:

- **Feelings of Frustration**: If you're feeling stuck or dissatisfied with your progress, acknowledge these feelings. Frustration is a sign that something needs to change. Do not bury these emotions;

let yourself sit with them and explore their deeper meaning.

- **Emotional Numbness**: A lack of emotional engagement can highlight areas that require renewed focus. If you find yourself feeling indifferent or disconnected from your self-love practices, take notice. This numbness can indicate that it's time to reassess your approach and find new ways to connect with yourself.

- **Lack of Motivation**: Reduced motivation may be a sign that your current self-love practices have become routine or ineffective. It's okay to feel unmotivated; this is a common experience. Use this opportunity to explore whether your self-care activities still serve you, or if they need to change to reignite your passion for self-love.

- **Reduced Personal Growth**: If you're no longer experiencing the growth you once did, it could indicate a plateau. This stagnation might appear as a feeling of repetitiveness in your routine or a lack of excitement about your self-improvement efforts. Think about whether you're challenging yourself or becoming too familiar with your comfort zone.

Spotting these signs early allows you to overcome plateaus proactively rather than waiting for feelings of burnout or despair to set in. These indicators are part of a cycle that prompts you to reassess your current situation and make improvements.

Implementing New Strategies

Once you've acknowledged that you're experiencing a plateau, it's time to implement new strategies to reignite personal growth.

Options you can explore:

- Step outside of your comfort zone and experiment with unconventional self-love practices that you've never tried before. You could try artistic expression, outdoor activities, or mindfulness practices that differ from your usual routine.

- Do something new to refresh your perspective on self-love. This could be a class, a new hobby, or setting a different personal challenge. Fresh experiences can boost your motivation and excitement, helping to pull you out of stagnation.

- Change can be a catalyst for growth. Identify areas in your self-care routine that feel stale or boring, and brainstorm ways to shake things up. You might adjust the time of day you practice self-care, choose a new environment for daily activities, or make use of different tools and prompts.

- Creative problem-solving comes from trying various self-love strategies. For example, if journaling feels monotonous, explore photography, art, or dance as alternative means of self-expression. Vary your approach, and you might experience unexpected breakthroughs in your emotional healing process.

- Define small, realistic goals that encourage progress to get you out of the plateau. Start with achievable tasks that focus on self-love, such as one affirming statement a day or dedicating ten minutes to gratitude. These attainable goals create a sense of accomplishment that motivates you to move forward.

- Take time to review your self-love progress thus far. What successes have you experienced? What challenges have you overcome? Can you identify a previous plateau and how you managed to grow again? Reflect on your achievements for a fresh perspective and a reminder of how far you've come.

These alternative strategies can renew your interest in self-love while encouraging flexibility and adaptability in your approach. Change will be key to moving on.

Getting External Support

Learning to love yourself is deeply personal, but that doesn't mean you have to go through the process alone. Other people can give you fresh perspectives and influence your ability to move forward during a plateau.

External support can look like:

1. Use professional resources, such as therapists or coaches, to get personalized guidance based on your unique challenges. Professionals can help you dig deeper into the underlying causes of your stagnation and devise personalized strategies for overcoming them. Support from someone knowledgeable helps you explore emotions and beliefs you may not have recognized previously.

2. Connecting with others experiencing similar growth can create a sense of camaraderie and understanding. Join support groups

or community workshops related to self-love for opportunities to share experiences and learn from others. Learning how others have worked through their plateaus develops motivation and offers fresh perspectives.

3. Participate in group discussions—in person or online—for new reflections and insights. Group settings can illuminate blind spots or unrecognized issues by giving you diverse viewpoints on common challenges. It also helps you feel less isolated and empowers you to stay the course.

4. Join group activities that focus on collaboration and self-improvement, such as book clubs, f, mindfulness classes, or wellness workshops. These environments can inspire new ideas and help you create connections that recharge your motivation and enthusiasm for self-care.

5. Don't hesitate to reach out to supportive friends or family members for feedback. Share your current experiences with them and invite them to provide insights. Sometimes, an external perspective can highlight patterns or behaviors you may be blind to, which offers new opportunities for growth.

External support is a tool that can enrich your self-love journey and help you in overcoming plateaus. Getting help demonstrates your commitment to self-discovery and improvement. Keep going; you've already made progress.

Patience and Acceptance

Have grace with yourself when you are faced with plateaus. It requires patience and acceptance to keep going. A mindset that acknowledges the natural ebb and flow of personal growth can change your experience.

Consider:

- Accept that plateaus are normal and a standard part of life. Remind yourself that growth comes with ups and downs that many others experience too. The reality of plateaus can lessen frustration and increase your ability to be patient with yourself.

- During challenging times, treat yourself with kindness and compassion. Keep in mind that everyone struggles with motivation or progress, and it's okay to feel this way. Self-compassion during hard moments helps you persevere and be resilient, helping you face plateaus with grace.

- Focus on the process, not just the outcome. Changing your emphasis from the end goal to the process itself helps you embrace the lessons and experiences you gain along the way, even during stagnation. Growth takes time and creates a more resilient mindset that allows you to appreciate every aspect of your life.

- Pay attention to your inner voice. If you notice negative self-talk or criticism bubbling up during a plateau, counteract those thoughts with affirming statements and strategies discussed in previous chapters. Reframe your thoughts to reflect your dedication to growing and nurturing self-love, even on days that feel stagnant.

- Reflect on how far you've come and the battles you've already won. Come up with rituals to celebrate your growth and progress, even if it feels small. These moments can motivate you to continue pressing forward.

Learning from the Transformation of Others

Other people can inspire your growth and self-love. There are many individuals who have overcome challenging pasts and emerged with renewed strength and self-acceptance; they are a source of insights, inspiration, and the resilience of the human spirit. Their stories highlight the possibilities of personal growth, regardless of a person's history. You can use the wisdom of others to enrich your life with self-love.

Role Models

Role models who embody self-love and resilience care all around you—in your community, at work, and in the media. Individuals who have transformed their lives despite facing challenges can be sources of inspiration and give you hope that change is possible for anyone. Let's take a look at a few people you may be familiar with.

Dwayne Johnson

Actor and mental health advocate Dwayne "The Rock" Johnson is often perceived as a confident and successful figure. He has openly discussed his battles with depression and mental health challenges. Growing up in a struggling family and encountering various obstacles throughout his life, Johnson faced moments of self-doubt and despair. He has used determination, support from loved ones, and a commitment to self-care to alter his mindset and embrace self-love. Johnson emphasizes the importance of addressing mental health openly and encourages others to get help when needed, demonstrating that strength lies in vulnerability.

Drew Barrymore

Drew Barrymore presents a compelling story of resilience and self-discovery. Known for her bubbly personality and successful career in Hollywood, she has openly faced her share of demons, including struggles with addiction and emotional turmoil from an early age. As a child star, the pressures of fame weighed heavily on Barrymore, leading to bouts of insecurity and challenges that could have easily pushed her over the edge. Introspection, therapy, and a commitment to transformation enabled Barrymore to find a path toward healing and self-compassion. She frequently emphasizes the importance of talking about mental health and encourages others to embrace their vulnerabilities. Barrymore has shown that true strength is found in confronting one's challenges and growing from them.

When studying role models, take the time to analyze their stories. Look beyond their successes and reflect on their past, struggles, and challenges to understand the strategies they used to overcome obstacles. Reflect on the techniques both Johnson and Barrymore used for self-affirmation and personal growth, and apply similar strategies in your life as you work on self-love. Seeing how these role models visualize their success can help you define what self-love means for you. Their triumphs demonstrate that developing self-worth is achievable and that your past does not determine your future.

The Stories of Others

Diverse personal narratives are all around you and can enrich your understanding of self-love. Books, podcasts, documentaries, and other media tend to share transformational journeys that reveal the complexities of personal growth. Immerse yourself in these stories to extract valuable lessons and insights.

You might want to read *Untamed* by Glennon Doyle, where she chronicles her path to self-discovery and empowerment. Doyle explores her life through authenticity and vulnerability, which may resonate with you, as she shares the challenges and breakthroughs in her pursuit of self-love. Her narrative can inspire you to confront your own barriers and nurture your self-worth.

Podcasts like *The Happiness Lab* with psychologist Dr. Laurie Santos discuss how different people have transformed their lives. These real-life stories highlight common themes, such as the role of community, the importance of self-acceptance, and the impact of embracing vulnerability. These discussions develop empathy and connection, reminding you that you are not alone in your struggles.

You can also watch documentaries like *Won't You Be My Neighbor?* about Fred Rogers, which provides insights into the power of self-love and kindness. His commitment to emotional well-being and self-acceptance in children and adults alike illustrates the lasting impact of compassion. Stories such as these can inspire you to adopt similar values and improve your ability to prioritize self-love.

As you consider various personal narratives, pay attention to the commonalities and unique approaches. Every path is different, and yet there is often a shared theme of resilience and growth in personal experiences.

Community Events

Make an effort to participate in community events centered on personal growth for a unique opportunity to connect with others who share similar goals. Workshops, support groups, and group activities can instill a sense of belonging and a shared purpose. These events enable collective learning where you can gather valuable insights from fellow participants.

More specifically, choose sessions focused on self-love and personal development. These gatherings usually include discussions that inspire accountability and motivation. For example, an online workshop could explain journaling exercises that help you explore your self-worth, share your reflections, and support one another in the process. This collective experience is infused with empathy and connection, reminding you that you are not alone as you grow.

With a bit of research, you may discover community events emphasizing creative outlets such as art therapy or yoga, which offer unique perspectives on self-love. These activities are cathartic and enable you to connect with like-minded individuals in a supportive environment. You might find that trying something outside your comfort zone is exactly what you need to motivate further change.

Peer Experiences

Open conversations with friends or family about their self-love experiences can be an insightful way to learn. Invite them to share their stories to add vulnerability to your discussions and create space for open exploration of emotions and challenges.

You can initiate dialogue with trusted peers by asking things like:

- What techniques or tools have helped you love yourself more?

- Have you faced any challenges in your journey to self-love? How did you overcome them?

- What inspired you to change your perspective on self-worth?

- How do you deal with plateaus and difficult days?

- What is one piece of advice you can give me as I work on self-love?

These open-ended questions evoke thoughtful responses and deeper connections because you get to know each other better. As you participate in these conversations, you'll likely discover that your peers have also faced obstacles and breakthroughs throughout their lives. Sharing these experiences creates opportunities to learn and refine strategies that you can apply in your life.

Diverse perspectives also broaden your understanding of self-love as a concept. Your peers may introduce you to fresh ideas or coping mechanisms that appeal to you. Be vulnerable and thank others for their input, as it allows everyone involved to feel seen and understood. Shared struggles can diminish feelings of isolation and remind you that the pursuit of self-love is a collective endeavor.

Key Takeaways

Unapologetic self-love is a lifelong commitment. You already have a range of tools and techniques to help you succeed. Self-love is about creating consistent habits, practicing self-compassion, and developing a growth mindset. Challenges will arise, but you can face them with grace and resilience.

Each step you take contributes to rewriting your story and strengthens your self-worth. You can create an inner sanctuary where joy, acceptance, and empowerment thrive, enabling you to reclaim your identity and celebrate it unabashedly. Trust in your capacity for growth and self-discovery; this story of unapologetic self-love is yours to shape, and it promises to be as fulfilling as it is transformative.

Chapter Eleven

Conclusion

The journey of self-love is never truly over. And you've already taken the first steps to making it your own! You are on an ongoing adventure filled with twists, turns, and newfound discoveries. Self-love is a lifelong commitment nurtured through dedication and practice, and the growth you experienced, whether monumental or subtle, is proof that each small step counts toward developing a healthier self-worth.

Embrace the idea that your story is filled with milestones and lessons. Each moment spent nurturing your inner voice, combating self-doubt, and allowing healing to take place is part of your growth. Even during the challenging stretches, you are changing and improving. You do not have to be perfect; focus on showing up for yourself, day after day, with compassion and understanding. Through these daily choices, you design a life filled with love, confidence, and joy. It's a commitment to yourself where you can watch as your growth unfolds in unexpected and beautiful ways.

Vulnerability—often seen as a weakness in our culture—is one of your most powerful tools for forming authentic connections. As you recognize vulnerability as a strength, you can develop stronger, more meaningful relationships rooted in trust and openness. Permit yourself to share your true identity and personality with others: your fears, your shortcomings, and your aspirations. This creates an inviting space for authenticity to thrive. Reflect on the connections you have made, and real relationships will blossom as you share your struggles and triumphs. These experiences make us human and create camaraderie with others facing similar challenges. Inspire each other to have empathy and compassion while forging a strong support system.

Don't be afraid to set healthy boundaries that protect your emotional well-being. Without boundaries, you risk compromising your needs, neglecting your self-care, and slipping back into past problems. Clear guidelines help you sustain respectful relationships while protecting your energy and mental health. These boundaries are not selfish; they are an essential act of self-care that reinforces your emotional health without guilt. Communicate your needs and limits clearly so that others can honor and respect your space, while you uphold their boundaries too. Valuing your needs sends a powerful message that you deserve love, respect, and consideration. Tap into the strength that comes from boundary-setting, and witness how it changes your relationships and improves your self-perception.

As you continue to love yourself unapologetically, take time to acknowledge and celebrate your progress. Commemorating achievements—whether big or small—gives your self-image a boost and motivates you to keep growing in self-love. Each step you take, each lesson you learn, and each moment of self-compassion is worthy of recognition. Never underestimate the power of celebrating even the smallest victories, as they remind you that every effort matters while creating a sense of accomplishment. As you grow more attuned to yourself, you will find it easier to face future challenges with renewed confidence and resilience.

You have the power to embrace your vulnerabilities, prioritize self-care, and honor your progress. Carry these lessons forward as you develop a flourishing relationship with yourself where you allow self-love, compassion, and authenticity to reign. Your journey has only just begun, and the best is yet to come!

A Note from Pages By The Lake, LLC

Thank you for spending time with one of our books. We hope it brought you insight, joy, or a few moments of escape.

If you enjoyed the read, please consider supporting the author by **"Writing a customer review at the site your purchased the book from."** Your feedback not only uplifts the writer—it helps other readers discover our books too.

Want more stories like this one? Visit us at **PagesByTheLake.com** to explore more titles from our growing collection.

—With gratitude,
Pages By The Lake, LLC
Where stories ripple into hearts and minds.

Chapter Twelve

References

Amore, P. (2023, March 27). The impact of social comparison on self-esteem and body image. *Softmind*. https://www.softmindindia.com/Blog/The-Impact-of-Social-Comparison-on-Self-Esteem-and-Body-Image

Balk, M. (2025, January 8). https://www.betterup.com/blog/personal-values-examples. *BetterUp*. https://www.betterup.com/blog/personal-values-examples

BetterHelp Editorial Team. (2025, February 28). *Impacts of social pressure*. BetterHelp. https://www.betterhelp.com/advice/general/how-does-social-pressure-impact-our-choices/

Brodsky, S. (2023, April 20). *11 ways to practice self-love that therapists swear by*. Wondermind. https://www.wondermind.com/article/self-love/

Carter, S. (2024, June 21). *Breaking free from perfectionism: 20 strategies for embracing imperfection and growth*. All Points North. https://apn.com/resources/breaking-free-from-perfectionism-20-strategies-for-embracing-imperfection-and-growth/

Chong, J. (2022, February 1). Low self-esteem: The role of social comparison. *The Skill Collective*. https://theskillcollective.com/blog/low-self-esteem-social-comparison

Cleveland Clinic. (2022, July 11). *How to set healthy boundaries in relationships*. Cleveland Clinic. https://health.clevelandclinic.org/how-to-set-boundaries

Coelho, S., & Smith, J. (2022, September 7). The benefits of self-compassion. *Psych Central*. https://psychcentral.com/blog/practicing-self-compassion-when-you-have-a-mental-illness

Connolly, M. (2021, October 20). *Let go of unrealistic expectations before they destroy your happiness*. Neways Somatic Psychotherapy & Coaching. https://newayscenter.com/let-go-unrealistic-expectations/

Cooks-Campbell, A. (2024, December 20). What self-love truly means and ways to cultivate it. *Betterup*. https://www.betterup.com/blog/self-love

Crego, A., Yela, J. R., Riesco-Matías, P., Gómez-Martínez, M.-Á., & Vicente-Arruebarrena, A. (2022). The benefits of self-compassion in mental health professionals: A systematic review of empirical research. *Psychology Research and Behavior Management, 15*, 2599–2620. https://doi.org/10.2147/PRBM.S359382

Engelstad, R. (2017, July 20). *How to avoid plateauing in the quest for personal growth*. Medium. https://medium.com/better-humans/how-to-avoid-plateauing-in-the-quest-for-personal-growth-d6ba98207ac7

Foy, C. (2023, February 3). *What are the effects of toxic relationships on mental health?* FHE Health. https://fherehab.com/learning/toxic-relationship-mental-health

Gillette, H. (2024, September 27). *Practicing self-love to improve well-being*. Psych Central. https://psychcentral.com/health/what-is-self-love-and-why-is-it-so-important

Godreau, J. (2024, February 2). *5 negative self-talk patterns: Origins and impacts on your mental health.* Mindful Health Solutions. https://mindfulhealthsolutions.com/5-negative-self-talk-patterns-origins-and-impacts-on-your-mental-health/

Grajek, M., Krupa-Kotara, K., Białek-Dratwa, A., Sobczyk, K., Grot, M., Kowalski, O., & Staśkiewicz, W. (2022). Nutrition and mental health: A review of current knowledge about the impact of diet on mental health. *Frontiers in Nutrition, 9.* https://doi.org/10.3389/fnut.2022.943998

Green, R. (2023, May 19). *The connection between mental health and physical health.* Verywell Mind. https://www.verywellmind.com/the-mental-and-physical-health-connection-7255857

Greenstein, L. (2017, August 9). *The power of a morning routine.* NAMI. https://www.nami.org/complimentary-health-approaches/the-power-of-a-morning-routine/

Gupta, S. (2023, November 21). *What is unresolved trauma?* Verywell Mind. https://www.verywellmind.com/unresolved-trauma-symptoms-causes-diagnosis-and-treatment-6753365

Halasgikar, M. (2025, January 14). Practical ways to build self-acceptance and let go of negativity. *BetterUp.* https://www.betterup.com/blog/self-acceptance

Hancock, J. (n.d.). *What are your values?* Mind Tools. https://www.mindtools.com/a5eygum/what-are-your-values

Holdsworth, K. (2023, March 2). *Self-Acceptance through creative activities.* Kay Holdsworth. https://www.kayholdsworth.com/self-acceptance-through-creative-activities/

Howard, Y. (2023, February 21). *The power of forgiveness in emotional healing*. Brighter Tomorrow Counseling. https://brightertomorrowth erapy.com/power-of-forgiveness/

Indurain, A. (n.d.). A guide for setting boundaries in relationships. *Lyra Health*. https://www.lyrahealth.com/blog/boundaries-in-relationships/

Klynn, B. (2024, November 28). Emotional regulation: Skills, exercises, and strategies. *BetterUp*. https://www.betterup.com/blog/emotional-r egulation-skills

Lefteris, P. (2023, July 11). *Embracing our unique-ness, celebrating the beauty of individuality*. Medi-um. https://medium.com/@Petros/embracing-our-uniqueness-celebra ting-the-beauty-of-individuality-60e3e99e5de2

Levy, T. (2025, January 15). *Why is forgiveness so important to emotional recovery from trauma and how do you get there?* Evergreen Psychotherapy Center. https://evergreenpsychotherapycenter.com/why-is-forgiveness-so-impo rtant-to-emotional-recovery-from-trauma-and-how-do-you-get-there/

Magalong, J. (n.d.). *Self-Blame: How to let go and find self-forgiveness*. Norooz Clinic. https://noroozclinic.com/self-blame-how-to-let-go-an d-find-self-forgiveness/

Maier, A. (2023, March 25). An antidote to self-blame. *Psychology To-day*. https://www.psychologytoday.com/us/blog/psychology-in-the-re al-world/202303/an-antidote-to-self-blame

Martin, S. (2024, June 3). Healing emotional wounds: 8 tips to help you begin. *Psychology To-*

day. https://www.psychologytoday.com/us/blog/conquering-codepe ndency/202406/healing-emotional-wounds-8-tips-to-help-you-begin

Maxwell Leadership. (2022, July 26). Goal vs. growth mindsets: How to avoid a personal growth and development plateau. *Maxwell Leadership*. https://www.maxwellleadership.com/blog/goal-versus-growt h-mindsets/

McGarvie, S. (2025a, January 9). *Emotional regulation: 5 evidence-based regulation techniques*. Positive Psychology. https://positi vepsychology.com/emotion-regulation/

McGarvie, S. (2025b, April 16). *The mind–body connection: Understanding their link*. Positive Psychology. https://positivepsychology.c om/body-mind-integration-attention-training/

Melissa Russell. (2024, May 30). Why celebrating small wins matters. *Harvard Summer School*. https://summer.harvard.edu/blog/why-cel ebrating-small-wins-matters/

Miller, K. (2020, March 13). *16 self-acceptance exercises & activities for adults*. Positive Psychology. https://positivepsychology.com/how-to -build-self-acceptance-activities-exercises/

Moore, M. (2022, October 11). *The good kind of vulnerability*. Psych Central. https://psychcentral.com/relationships/the-good-kind-of-v ulnerability

Muscaritoli, M. (2021). The impact of nutrients on mental health and well-being: Insights from the literature. *Frontiers in Nutrition, 8*(8). https://doi.org/10.3389/fnut.2021.656290

Musu, S. (2022, September 6). Where do I begin my self-love journey? *The Equality Institute.* https://www.equalityinstitute.org/blog/where-do-i-begin-my-self-love-journey

Neff, K. D. (2009). The role of self-compassion in development: A healthier way to relate to oneself. *Human Development, 52*(4), 211–214. https://doi.org/10.1159/000215071

Northwestern Medicine. (2022, December). *Health benefits of having a routine.* Northwestern Medicine. https://www.nm.org/healthbeat/healthy-tips/health-benefits-of-having-a-routine

Pearson, M., & Wilson, H. (2024). Guiding clients towards self-kindness and acceptance: Wrestling with the inner critic. *Psychotherapy and Counselling Journal of Australia, 12*(2). https://doi.org/10.59158/001c.123356

Perry, E. (2022a, February 11). Overcome self-doubt (once and for all?): 8 tips to move forward. *BetterUp.* https://www.betterup.com/blog/overcoming-self-doubt

Perry, E. (2022b, September 19). How self-compassion and motivation will help achieve your goals. *BetterUp.* https://www.betterup.com/blog/self-compassion-and-motivation

Prucha, D. (2024, September 3). Breaking free from perfectionism: A practical guide. *Lyra Health.* https://www.lyrahealth.com/blog/perfectionism/

Psychological benefits of routines. (2024, September 19). WebMD. https://www.webmd.com/mental-health/psychological-benefits-of-routine

Psychologs. (2024, February 28). *Breaking the cycle of self-doubt and negative thinking*. Psychologs. https://www.psychologs.com/breaking-the-cycle-of-self-doubt-and-negative-thinking/

Ramar, K., Malhotra, R. K., Carden, K. A., Martin, J. L., Abbasi-Feinberg, F., Aurora, R. N., Kapur, V. K., Olson, E. J., Rosen, C. L., Rowley, J. A., Shelgikar, A. V., & Trotti, L. M. (2021). Sleep is essential to health: An American Academy of sleep medicine position statement. *Journal of Clinical Sleep Medicine, 17*(10), 2115–2119. https://doi.org/10.5664/jcsm.9476

Raypole, C. (2022, July 26). *How to hack your hormones for a better mood*. Healthline. https://www.healthline.com/health/happy-hormone

Reid, S. (2025, March 13). *Setting healthy boundaries in relationships*. HelpGuide.org. https://www.helpguide.org/relationships/social-connection/setting-healthy-boundaries-in-relationships

Reynolds, C. (2015, October 21). Practicing gratitude as a bridge to self-compassion. *Zest Infusion*. https://zestinfusion.com.au/practicing-gratitude-as-a-bridge-to-self-compassion/

Riopel, L. (2019, September 14). *17 self-awareness tests, activities, and exercises*. Positive Psychology. https://positivepsychology.com/self-awareness-exercises-activities-test/

Scott, E. (2023, September 26). *How to use assertive communication*. Verywell Mind. https://www.verywellmind.com/learn-assertive-communication-in-five-simple-steps-3144969

Selhub, E. (2022, September 18). Nutritional psychiatry: Your brain on food. *Harvard Health*. https://www.health.harvard.edu/blog/nutrition al-psychiatry-your-brain-on-food-201511168626

Seppala, E. (2014, May 8). *The scientific benefits of self-compassion*. Stanford Medicine. https://ccare.stanford.edu/uncategorized/the-scientific -benefits-of-self-compassion-infographic/

Shah, S. (2022, December 9). *How societal pressure affects our mental health and happiness*. Medium. https://medium.com/change-your-mind/societ al-pressure-and-shocking-impact-on-our-day-to-day-lives-c2aa30688c78

Shah, U. (2024, April 2). *How to be authentic and open to get what you want in a relationship*. MyWellbeing. https://mywellbeing.com/therapy-101/ how-to-be-authentic-in-a-relationship

Sonder Wellness. (2021, June 22). Healthy risk-taking: 10 simple ways to practice vulnerability. *Sonder Wellness*. https://www.sonderwellness.co m/blog/2021/06/22/vulnerability/

Stanborough, R. J. (2023, June 5). *How to change negative thinking with cognitive restructuring*. Healthline. https://www.healthline.com/health/ cognitive-restructuring

Staples, L. (2021, August 18). The real reason to avoid self-judgment. *Psychology Today*. https://www.psychologytoday.com/us/blog/make-up -with-your-mind/202108/the-real-reason-to-avoid-self-judgment

Streep, P. (2018, January 10). Tackling self-blame and self-criticism: 5 strategies to try. *Psychology Today*. https://www.psychologytoday.com/us/blog/tech-support/201801 /tackling-self-blame-and-self-criticism-5-strategies-to-try

Sutton, J. (2021, July 6). *How to perform assertiveness training: 6 exercises.* Positive Psychology. https://positivepsychology.com/assertiveness-traini ng/

Sutton, J. (2022, January 28). *How to use mindfulness therapy for anxiety: 15 exercises.* Positive Psychology. https://positivepsychology.com/mindf ulness-for-anxiety/

Tartakovsky, M. (2022, June 16). *How to relinquish unrealistic expectations: 4 tips.* Psych Central. https://psychcentral.com/lib/how-to-relinquish-u nrealistic-expectations

The power of saying no. (2023, June 19). *Psychology To-day.* https://www.psychologytoday.com/us/blog/mind-matters-from-m enninger/202111/the-power-of-saying-no

The psychology of social comparison. (n.d.). *Click2Pro.* https://click2pr o.com/blog/psychology-of-social-comparison

Yildiz, M. (2023, January 24). *Here's how I defeated societal pressures creatively to maintain my sanity.* Medium. https://medium.com/sensible-biohacking-transhumanism/heres-how-i-d efeated-societal-pressures-assertively-and-creatively-to-maintain-my-sanit y-9cbb75d22331

Zoppi, L. (2024, January 22). *Is it normal to talk to yourself?* Medical News Today. https://www.medicalnewstoday.com/articles/talking-to-yourself